PSYCHOLOGY OF MONEY

How to Discover Your Midas Touch

ilya julius teplitsky

Julius Books • Oakland, Califonia

PSYCHOLOGY OF *MONEY*
How to Discover Your *Midas Touch*
By Ilya Julius Teplitsky, MFT

Published by Julius Books
2868 Carmel Street
Oakland, CA 94602-3450, USA

Unattributed quotations are by Ilya J. Teplitsky

First Printing in 2004

ISBN 0-9759099-0-8

Text and cover design by Jonathan Gullery,
Budget Book Design, USA

Printed in the United States of America by United Graphics Incorporated, USA

Money has a mystique of its own, and your ability to earn a living most often has little correlation with your talents, intelligence, education or dedication.

Other forces are at play that influence, frequently even determine, your financial successes and failures.

Each of us carries within a unique ability to generate prosperity. You can discover yours on the following pages.

Acknowledgements

I would like to express my gratitude to the hundreds of my clients and students who shared with me the stories of their financial successes and failures, and also to:

My editor and consultant, George Cohen, who shocked me with his unsurpassed dedication to the improvement of the book's title, content, structure, tone, flow and style; and who shared with me his encyclopedic knowledge of financial psychotherapy;

My editor, Lisa Camasi, for her help in creating the book structure and improving its grammar; as well as for her gentle determination to reduce my over generalizations and outrageous statements that could have offended too many readers;

My editors, Zoe Newman and Helene Miller, for putting the final touches on the book's content and grammar;

My lifelong friend, Jaffa de la Fontain, for sharing with me her expertise in designing the book cover;

My parents, for their most valuable moral and material support for, as well as for their most formidable resistance to, this book's production;

And my best friend, Eliane Walis, for helping me to significantly improve the book's readability and eliminate a lot of "extra" material; and also for inspiring me to study the art of being present.

Disclaimer

This book has been written to provide information on the relationship between psychology and wealth acquisition. However, it is not designed to provide any financial, psychological or legal advice.

No book, even this one, can automatically bring you wealth without you taking the appropriate actions to acquire it. *No financial strategies, including those discussed here, can guarantee success.* All good things in life require either effort or money, or both, and *there will always be risks involved.* This book may help you find your path of least resistance to prosperity and significantly reduce the possibility of financial loss. Nevertheless, it is not the author or publisher, but the readers themselves who will be responsible for the successes or failures resulting from implementing the book's general ideas into their specific actions.

The author and the publisher shall have neither liability nor responsibility to any person or entity with respect to any losses or damaged caused, or alleged to have been caused, directly or indirectly by this book's content.

Introduction

My own quest for unlimited personal freedom, meaningful work and financial success was typical for a person going through mid-life crisis. I quit my lucrative employment and embarked upon the exciting and risky journey of a small business owner.

In spite of the spectacular professional success I enjoyed almost from the start (beginner's luck), financial success continued to elude me. Two advanced degrees, a psychotherapy license and years of experience did not make much difference. Marsha Sinetar's principle, *Do What You Love, the Money Will Follow*, did not work for me. Nor did it work for most of my clients, students, teachers and associates.

Eventually, I discovered that many, perhaps most, geniuses who found their rightful place in history books could not generate sufficient income by doing what they loved and had talents for, especially in the beginning of their career. For example, Einstein worked as a patent clerk for years; Mozart lived and died in poverty; and Spinoza earned a living as an oculist. The most prolific East Indian writer, Rabindranath Tagore, as popular among one billion Hindus as Shakespeare is in the West, was unable to support himself with his writing. Instead, his father provided for him and his family.

For most of us, financal success has very little correlation with our talents, education, intelligence or even tremendous and sustained efforts. In fact, millions of people generate very substantial income by engaging in occupations in which they are mediocre at best.

I have witnessed numerous failures of my clients and associates to get rich by using witchcraft, gambling, financial speculations or marrying into riches. Living economically and saving pennies to get by does not work either. Even after cutting all expenses to a bare minimum, for most people these expenses would still exceed the income.

None of the popular methodologies of making money presented by Napoleon Hill, Anthony Robbins, Suze Ormand or Deepak Chopra (to name just a few) have worked for most of those who tried to apply them in their lives. However, *such methodologies did work for those who created them, as well as for a few of their followers*. This insight was my most crucial realization in my search for financial freedom. This realization enabled me to translate my personal and professional experience into the principles of the *Psychology of Money*.

Case Studies

Numerous case histories are presented throughout the book that include the lives of historical figures, as well as ordinary people from all walks of life. Most of the names of individuals who participated in these studies have been changed and their stories slightly altered to preserve confidentiality. Any resemblance of case studies to the life of the reader or reader's associates is purely coincidental.

Contents

Part I

THE MIDAS TOUCH

DEFINITIONS
AND PRINCIPLES

CHAPTER ONE

Principles of Prosperity

The Philosopher's Stone

According to J.K. Rowling's *Harry Potter and the Sorcerer's Stone*, there was a magic stone that would give immortality to its owner. This Sorcerer's Stone is indeed a product of imagination, but not of J.K. Rowling's. For about a thousand years, alchemists of Europe and the Middle East not only believed in such a stone, but actively tried to find or manufacture it. This Philosopher's Stone (called Sorcerer's Stone by J.K. Rowling) could also vest its owner with the power to transform basic metals into gold. The owner of the Sorcerer's (Philosopher's) Stone in the film, Nicholas Flanell, was not a fictional character. This alchemist did exist, and many of his contemporaries believed that he actually possessed such a Philosopher's Stone that enabled him to achieve immortality and transform basic metals into gold. Nicholas Flanell mysteriously disappeared more than two centuries ago, but his legend is as alive today as it was in his time. Quite a few students of metaphysical arts still believe that this Stone is well hidden in some exotic location and seek it out.

Besides the Philosopher's Stone, there are other magical objects that humanity has tried to discover or produce since time immemorial. The human race has been obsessed with special "living" water and the fountain of youth to cure all illnesses

13

and extend life indefinitely. At various times, the unicorn's horn, magic swords and wands, as well as prosperity carpets, stirred the imagination of human race. The all-powerful and all-magical Holy Grail, depicted in *Excalibur*, is not just a creation of modern cinematography. It came to us from a medieval legend, believed with such conviction that many a knight went on a quest to find it.

Just a few years ago, many considered Prozac a cure-all for every common stress or sadness, or Pritkin's diet as a means to help everybody lose weight. Most recently, Viagra has been presented as a solution for all (or at least most) male sexual dysfunctions.

It is so comforting to believe in a pill to cure all illnesses, or a magical stone able to help you instantaneously get rich.

Unfortunately, this cannot be. No such magic pill will be ever produced and no stone of instantaneous riches will ever be found. And no system of prosperity, even created by the most brilliant minds of the century, will work for the vast majority of those who read their books. Such methodologies of prosperity did work for those who created them and for a few of their followers, but they are not appropriate for most of us.

We all are different in our backgrounds, talents, abilities, strengths, weaknesses, personal preferences, etc. There is no system of prosperity that fits us all.

This book *will not* teach you my system of prosperity, which works well for me, and for a few others like me, but almost certainly will not work for you. However, *this book will assist you in creating your own personal strategy to acquire wealth, or at least help you learn how to generate sufficient income with minimal effort. This strategy will be based on your uniqueness, such as your family of origin and personal history. Ultimately, it will be your own unique strategy that will work for you and for no one else!*

A Carrot before the Horse

Money acts as a carrot, dangled before the horse, yet out of its reach. No matter how fast the horse will run after this carrot, it will never get it.

For many of us, our need for money is the best motivation to act, compete, create, learn and make our contribution to life. Sometimes, money is the only thing that can motivate us at all. In spite of our intelligence, we are still biological organisms, and all biological organisms can act vigorously, courageously, consistently and efficiently only when motivated by instincts, such as hunger, fear or desire to procreate.

Besides being biological organisms, we are also social beings that can be motivated by a number of other things besides our biological drives. One of the strongest of such motivators is money, which is a metaphor for a great many things, including our biological needs for food, shelter, security and procreation.

Regardless of all the explanations, the horse will never reach this bloody carrot, no matter how fast it runs after it. Of course this horse will be fed at the end of the day, but it will not eat the carrot, which will be used as the horse motivator again the next day, and so on, until the horse gets old and retires. All the horses will be treated almost equally at the end of the day. Well, the horses that run faster after the carrot will get a bit more attention and affection, but not enough to justify superior efforts.

Most of us, traditionally employed, have experienced that raises, promotions and bonuses are rarely proportional to our efforts, and those who try very hard, usually get just a little bit more, and occasionally a lot less due to their co-workers' jealousy and their managers' insecurities. Of course, those consistently working hard for promotions eventually get them. However, hard work and dedication usually are only small components of their success. They normally have other qualities that get them promoted, like intelligence, social skills, con-

15

nections, youth, good looks and plain luck.

Many small business owners believe that just by working hard they can succeed. Unfortunately, it takes a lot more than hard work to achieve success, and with hard work alone any business will either fail or lead a meager existence.

And what happens when you do succeed? Your expenses go up. You feel that you and your family deserve greater rewards for hard work and deprivation. Since no one provides you with such rewards, you then have to reward yourself with little (and not so little) treats here and there. Besides, making more money, you are in a different league now, and must maintain an appropriate lifestyle to fit into your new position. Guess what? After ever mounting expenses, the money that you make is rarely enough, and the horse must run ever faster after the carrot, until it falls and can run no more.

How come some people do win this game? They still run, but no longer after the carrot. They run for exercise instead. Paradoxically, such people do get the carrot, but not by running harder or faster. They get this carrot by applying their *Midas Touch*, discussed in the next chapter.

Note: Please, do not ask who placed this carrot before the horse. I do not know why we always have to run after money, never getting quite enough of it no matter how hard we try. I do not know who made it so. Was it God, the Devil, evolution, DNA, human nature, all the above, some of the above, or none of the above? I do not know who made it so. I only know that it is so.

Money as an Educational Game

Money is an educational game that forces you to learn about yourself and the world around you. Money has a special magic, and the monetary exchange follows its own laws, most of which you cannot learn in any textbooks on economics. These laws are subtle, difficult to see with your naked eye.

Incidentally, "In the sweat of thy face, shalt thou earn your daily bread" (as translated from the Russian Bible, Genesis, Chapter 3) is not one of them! Besides, *the rules of this game of money are not constant. They change from person to person, and may vary in different periods of your own life.* But do not despair. Not only is it quite possible to learn the rules of this game, but it is also a relatively easy thing to do, if you possess two particular qualities of character, and superior intelligence is not one of them. These critical qualities are detachment and the power of observation. Your ability to observe life as it is, and to accept the obvious existence of what you might consider improbable, impossible or undesirable, without allowing other people to affect your judgment.

The Four Noble Truths of Buddha

The principle of detachment discussed above is one of the foundations of Buddhism. Below are two common interpretations of Buddha's *Four Noble Truths*. Each of them is a superb example of Buddha's power of observation; each provides a solution in many areas of our lives, including money.

Here is the first interpretation of Buddha's teaching:

- Life is suffering
- It does not have to be so
- There is a way out of suffering
- This way is the Eight-fold Path

(The Eight-fold Path refers to a particular way of life that includes right views, right resolve, right speech, right action, right livelihood, right effort, right mindfulness and right concentration.)

And here is how I apply this interpretation in my book:

- Lack of money is a cause of suffering.
- It does not have to be so.
- It is possible to overcome financial limitations.
- This can be done by discovering your *Midas Touch*.

The second interpretation of Buddha's teaching is more specific, but it offers essentially the same solution to human problems:

- Life is suffering
- The cause of suffering is our attachments.
- To be free of suffering, we must let go of attachments.
- This can be achieved through the Eight-fold Path.

And here is how I apply the second interpretation in this book.

- Lack, or perceived lack, of money creates suffering.
- The cause of this suffering is attachment to dysfunctional financial strategies.
- To stop suffering, one must let go of these attachments.
- And replace them with the *Midas Touch*.

So, let's discuss this all powerful and mysterious *Midas Touch* in the next chapter.

CHAPTER TWO

The Midas Touch

The Legend

Once upon a time there was a king in Phrygia, located on the territory of present-day Turkey. His name was Midas. Almighty Zeus, the ruler of the Greek gods, loved Midas above all people, so he gave him the ability to transform all matter into gold by a single touch. Since then, the ability to amass large amounts of gold or generate large sums of money has come to be called the *Midas Touch*.

By observing about a thousand of my clients, students and associates, I have arrived to the conclusion that everyone possesses a *Midas Touch*, which is a unique ability to generate money rapidly, efficiently and with minimal effort. Ironically, this *Midas Touch* rarely manifests itself through one's career or other professional endeavors and may have very little correlation with one's talents, education, intelligence or superior efforts. Instead, one's fortune is often found in many other domains, which may include relationships, inheritance, real estate, investing, gambling, collecting art, relocation, etc. The list of possibilities is endless.

The Paradox of Diminishing Returns

Like most people, you probably believe that your financial rewards should be proportional to your efforts, as well as to your innate talents and intelligence, and that with more education, or more dedication and a bit of luck, you will eventually receive greater financial reward.

If you own a business, you—like most of us—probably believe that the more you invest in your business, the greater your financial return will be.

Similarly, most investors believe that buying more shares of a stock or diversifying (buying more shares of a wider variety of stocks) will produce greater profits.

This belief that greater effort or larger investment will always produce greater result is merely a myth, even though many believe it to be true. Even if you accept this myth as a general principle of prosperity, you should still keep in mind that all general principles have one thing in common: for each general principle, the opposite could also be equally true.

Indeed, in the beginning financial results are usually proportionate to our efforts, and the more talented, better educated and more industrious do earn a lot more than the dull, the ignorant and the lazy. However, as you can see in Fig. 1, the correlation between effort and financial reward eventually changes. At a certain point, more effort, or more investment, or greater talent, or better education will not produce greater financial results. So, no matter how hard you try, the results will remain the same. If you continue to increase your effort, you may even experience a paradox: more effort will produce smaller results and eventually may ruin your business or get you fired from your job. Naturally, when you overwork, you are tired, frustrated, angry, resentful and occasionally just plain crazy. Your productivity falls, you begin to make serious and costly mistakes and lose your ability to relate to your clients, customers, partners and co-workers. All of this will surely lead to employment termination or business collapse.

The phenomenon discussed above is an example of what is called sometimes *the law of diminishing returns*, which operates in any kind of human activity, as shown in Fig. 1.

Take aerodynamics for example. The velocity of airplanes cannot exceed a certain limit. Once this limit is reached, any additional fuel you will burn to increase the speed will result only in an equal increase of the air resistance, which will maintain the speed. If you persevere in burning more fuel, the air resistance will eventually break the plane's structure, and you will crash.

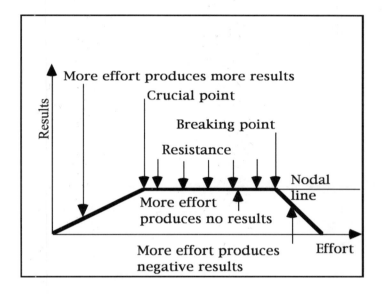

Fig. 1

The above diagram also describes various naturally occurring phenomena. The transformation of pure water into steam is another example. When water is heated in an open container, its temperature will increase only to 100° Centigrade (the boiling point), and no amount of heat will make it any hotter. The water will continue boiling at 100° Centigrade for a while until it all becomes steam, as shown on Fig. 2. It evaporates in the same manner as opportunities, clients, projects, etc. will disappear in any business or career, if you persevere with your effort beyond the breaking point.

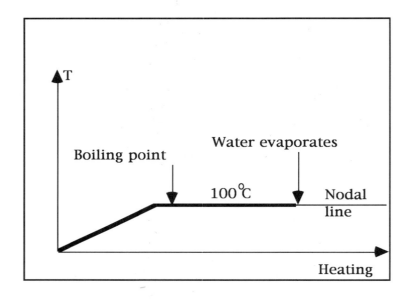

Fig. 2

In all the above examples, we are dealing with the universal *law of transformation of quantity into quality* that governs many, if not all, natural and technological processes. You can observe the manifestation of this law in the melting of metals, in the transformation of various substances in chemical reactions and in nuclear fusion, to name just a few. This law also applies to many biological processes, such as the transformation of a caterpillar into a butterfly, or an egg into a chicken. Our personal transformation from a fetus into a human being is also governed by this law. A well-known German philosopher and revolutionary, Frederick Engels, applied this *law of transformation of quantity into quality* to the 19th century capitalist system. He believed that the accumulation of massive changes in the capitalist system would eventually bring it to its inevitable crisis. In this crisis, the capitalist system would evaporate like water into steam, and a new political system (communist according to Engels) will emerge.

As we all know, Engels political predictions were mostly inaccurate, and our capitalist system, imperfect as it may seem, still is very much alive.

Nevertheless, the law of the *transformation of quantity into quality* may still apply to many income-producing activities in our capitalist economy, like employment, business and investment.

Suppose for a year or two your ever increasing efforts have ceased producing greater financial results. This usually means that you have reached Engels' *nodal line* (Fig. 1), or simply gotten stuck, if you prefer a more common language. On this *nodal line*, no matter how hard you try the financial results will remain the same. Applying greater effort on your job or pouring more money into your business will act upon your income producing-activity like additional heat acts upon already boiling water. This may bring your job or business to a *breaking point*. Then, your greater effort will begin producing negative results. If you still persevere in applying more effort, chances are that your business or your job will evaporate like water heated beyond the boiling point. Therefore, *if you have been trying to increase your income for months or even years in vain—stop!* You may have to pull back and do some restructuring, or perhaps do something else instead of what you have been doing till now.

Do not despair though. Even in the above case, your situation is far from hopeless, and the solution will be discussed on the following pages.

In some occupations or businesses the *nodal line* will be higher, but the same formula will still apply: Once the limit is reached, more effort will not produce greater results, as shown in Fig. 3.

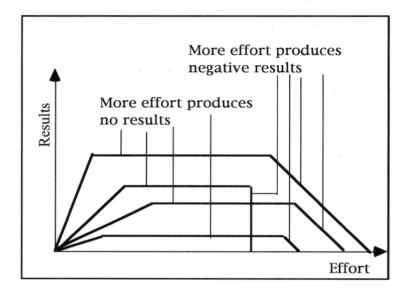

Fig. 3

The Midas Touch Formula

In the early nineties, I began teaching a class, *Discover Your Life Purpose*. Already in my first class, I realized that my students did not have the problem of not knowing their purpose in life. Most of them have known it for years. Their problem was lack of money.

So, I wrote the following formula on the board:

$$\frac{\$ \text{ total income}}{\text{Number of Hours}} = \$ \text{ per hour}$$

According to this formula, most Americans were earning $15-20 per hour in the late 1990s.

Then I asked my students to remember at least one activity that produced substantially more dollars per hour than what they earned in their jobs or businesses. The results were astounding and are presented in the following case studies. Some of the events presented below occurred after the class.

Case Study: Fastia

Fastia was a social worker, earning about $19 per hour. Her job took all her energy. Overworked, tired, frustrated and resentful, she only vaguely remembered that she had bought a few mutual funds with a policy of a monthly automatic withdrawal. Her investment had grown, and by the year 1997, her accumulated mutual fund assets were greater than all she had earned during the long and hard years of her employment. All she had to do to make money in mutual funds was to spend about an hour or two selecting the funds that felt right to her and filling out the appropriate investment forms. Her profit was truly astounding even in the context of the robust stock market of the 1990s! Probably, she would have made a lot more money if she had spent as much effort on learning about the investment world as she had on doing her job.

Case Study: Jennifer

Jennifer was a receptionist, earning $15 per hour. When she was laid off, she had nothing to do, except read and go to garage sales, where she began buying old stuff, reselling it later on. She would buy silverware, antiques, works of art, etc., for a few dollars and sell it for a lot more. Jennifer had no prior knowledge of antiques, no previous sales experience. Nevertheless, success came to her without effort. She simply possessed an innate intuitive ability to find treasures in others' old junk. Currently, she is making a lot more money in her new business than on her previous job—often as much as twenty times more per hour.

Case study: Laura

Laura was happily married with two children. She supported her family's modest lifestyle by her employment as a social worker. When the children had grown and left the house, Laura decided to pursue her life passion. She had always loved organizing parties and special events and enjoyed serving exquisite gourmet dishes. So, after quitting her job, she started her own catering company in her garage. Soon, managing her company became Laura's greatest passion—her true mission in life. The business developed rapidly. Within a year, Laura was already organizing and managing large catered events involving hundreds, occasionally thousands, of people. Her events were attended by mayors, state governors, and once by a Vice President of the United States. Laura worked long hours, but it did not feel like work. Instead, it felt like a day-long party, which it was. Her income was astronomical, especially when compared with her previous social worker's salary of $18 per hour.

Note. Do not attempt to reproduce the results described in the above cases. The *Midas Touch* is a unique personal quality that we all are born with. *It is different for each of us!* I am convinced that Fastia would not even consider going to garage sales, which worked so well for Jennifer. And neither of them would be able to reproduce Laura's success in catering.

Midas Touch Diagram

The diagram, shown on Fig. 4, is based on the successful experiences of some of my students who have discovered and implemented their *Midas Touch*. It shows the effort/reward ratio that you are likely to experience when involved in an activity related to your *Midas Touch*.

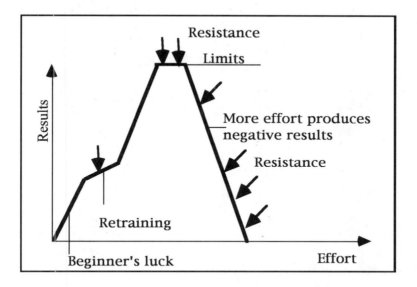

Fig. 4

You can see that this diagram is much steeper than the two previous ones, showing far greater financial results for your efforts. It also shows that you will experience *beginner's luck* at the very start of the process. Then resistance will slow you down for a short while, after which the steep ascent to financial prosperity will continue until you reach your limit. Usually, this limit is so far above your present expectations that you may never even try to reach it. However, a few daring souls who will go all the way will eventually discover the limit of their *Midas Touch*. If they try to go beyond this limit they will encounter a most formidable resistance which will cause their inevitable downfall.

Let's examine some of the *Midas Touch* qualities in the next chapter.

CHAPTER THREE

Beginner's Luck Forever

The Ultimate Equality

The sun does not discriminate between the righteous and the wicked. It shines equally for all, and anyone born under the sun has the right to enjoy and prosper under it. You do not have to do or to be anything special to deserve the sunlight. To enjoy it is your birthright. The same is true for your *Midas Touch*. It is like an innate talent. You are simply born with it, and therefore do not need to do anything to deserve it. However, as it is true for every talent, your *Midas Touch* will improve with practice.

Beginner's Luck

When you begin practicing your *Midas Touch*, you are usually successful from the start. When you deliberately or accidentally get involved in an activity directly related to your *Midas Touch*, your actions will often bring good financial results. Even though you may have no appropriate education or experience, you still succeed, as if the universe supports your efforts. People call it *beginner's luck*. However, this *beginner's luck* phenomenon is not luck at all, but an indication that you have discovered your *Midas Touch*. Luck is unpredictable, transient, and hard to reproduce reliably. Your *Midas Touch* is not. You can expect that such pseudo "luck" will continue for a long while, as long as you are engaged in the same activity that produced it originally.

Defying the Statistical Probability

Anything related to the *Midas Touch* defies the laws of statistical probability. A statistical analysis may very well indicate that you will lose money big time when gambling, as happens to almost everyone who tries this risky enterprise. The whole business of gambling is designed to insure such results. Nevertheless, if gambling is the domain of your *Midas Touch*, you will consistently make money at it, in spite of the impossible odds.

Case study: Patricia

Patricia attended horse races for the first and only time in her life on her fiftieth birthday. She had never gambled before, or even been to Las Vegas, Reno, Atlanta or any other gambling establishments anywhere. Her only prior experience with horses was riding one for a few hours. On her first bet, she won big. Her second bet also brought her about 1000% return on her investment, and by the end of the day at the races, she had won on all of her bets. Patricia did not make a huge sum of money on her bets, since her bets were very small. Nevertheless, overall she made about 500% return of her investment.

Next year, Patricia went to Las Vegas, where she discovered that her success at the horse races was not accidental. Her winnings at slot machines were also impressive. As with the races, Patricia did not make much, since she risked only a few dollars at a time. Nevertheless, her results were spectacular on a percentage basis.

It appeared that Patricia had special ability to make money in gambling. Unfortunately, she lacked external reinforcement of this innate ability of hers, as well as the skill or guidance to recognize it in herself. As a result, Patricia did not explore gambling as a means of making money. Like most of us, she needed acknowledgment and support to develop her innate abilities.

Without such support, Patricia's successes at the races and casinos soon faded from her memory.

Boom and Bust

Very few things in life are 100% consistent and reliable. The *Midas Touch* never works like a clock with totally predictable results. There will be occasional periods when even your *Midas Touch* will stop transforming basic metals into gold, and you will experience only modest returns or even losses. Such losses—if they occur—are usually not substantial, and are soon forgotten, when another cycle of good fortune begins. However, these inconsistencies of the *Midas Touch* usually evoke inner and outer resistance, as shown on Fig. 4 in the previous chapter (a single arrow on the left side of the diagram).

Resistance

Such resistance usually arises when you compare the inconsistency of your *Midas Touch* with the perceived security of your 9-to-5 job. The perception of job security compared to the relative insecurity of the *Midas Touch* is an illusion. In reality, your *Midas Touch* will always remain with you, while you will probably quit jobs or get laid off numerous times during your career. In all probability, there will be periods of six months or longer between jobs, during which you will live on your unemployment or your savings.

When you decide to explore your *Midas Touch*, you will encounter external resistance from your loving spouse or partner, as well as your well-meaning parents, and supportive friends. They will remain unimpressed with your initial success and will try to convince you to give up your pipe dreams and keep your day job or maintain "business as usual". This usually means that they depend on you to continue performing your role in their life, and they fear that if you change, even for the better, you may refuse or become unable to continue playing this role.

This fear is powerful and may resonate with your own fears of success or failure. (This topic will be addressed in greater detail in Chapter Sixteen.) In the vast majority of cases, what those close to us want from us most is *consistency* (even if this is the consistency of failure and suffering, rather than success.

Education and Retraining

Even with "beginner's luck," you may have to get some education, training and experience in the activity related to your *Midas Touch*. Most likely though, you will need very little preparation, especially when compared to all the years of schooling and "indentured servitude" that you have to go through in most professions.

Case study: Laura

As we discussed in Chapter Two, Laura was a social worker who became the successful owner of a catering company. It took Laura four years of college to get her Master's Degree in social work, and two years of supervised internship to get licensed, just to earn $19 per hour. (Nineteen dollars an hour was worth a lot more ten years ago than it is now.) In comparison, during her first year of catering, Laura's income increased to several hundred per hour. She is probably making a few thousand per hour now. Perhaps Laura's success was exceptional, but what about Jennifer?

Case study: Jennifer

We have already discussed Jennifer in Chapter Two. She was a receptionist who began to earn a living by reselling the items she bought at garage sales. As a receptionist, Jennifer did not have any formal training, but it took her years of working for minimal wages to get to the point of making $15 per hour. When she reached that point, she was laid off. In her garage sales enterprise, she had no formal resale training, yet she started making $50 per hour with only a few weeks of experience.

The Limits of the Midas Touch

Even with the *Midas Touch*, the potential for income increase is not infinite, and there are limits on how much you can earn even under the best of circumstances. (See Fig. 4.) Some people are born with the potential to become billionaires, others to live comfortably on a small budget, and many with the potential for upper middle class incomes. The limits of the *Midas Touch* can be compared with the role of innate physical limitations in sports. With sufficient effort, almost everyone can become an athlete. Only a very few however have the innate ability to become world champions, a feat physically impossible for the rest of us no matter how hard we may try.

As shown on Fig. 4, the limits of financial success achievable with the *Midas Touch* are usually very high. Most likely, yours are much higher than you can presently imagine. It is perfectly fine if you are not ambitious enough to ever try reaching these limits. You do not have too. Most probably, you will be able to reach your financial goals long before you even come close to the limits of your *Midas Touch*.

In rare cases however, these innate financial limitations can be set very low. Raising them higher may not only be desirable but even necessary for some. Chapters Fifteen, Sixteen, Nineteen, Twenty and Twenty-One will deal with this matter.

The Path of Least Resistance

Practicing your *Midas Touch* is never difficult, and the financial rewards frequently come with minimal effort. You will discover that life supports you, as if you swim downstream in the river of life, with the river providing most of the movement. Some people feel compelled however to continue working very hard even after they have implemented their *Midas Touch* in their work or business. Such individuals are so accustomed to hard work that they cannot imagine living without it.

Money and Talent

You have probably wondered how and why some individuals in your profession, who are not nearly as talented, experienced, educated or dedicated as you, are able to earn so much more than you do. There is a simple answer: they are practicing their *Midas Touch*, and you are not. Most often, your *Midas Touch* is unrelated to any unique and superior skill that you have developed in the course of your life. Often, one's technical skills and mastery in the occupations related to one's *Midas Touch* are average, frequently even below average.

Case study: Elaine

Elaine was exceptionally talented in two fields: acting and bodywork. She achieved considerable recognition as an actress in her youth, but acting was always a great struggle financially. In her thirties, she started doing Breema Bodywork, which is a unique healing practice dedicated to balancing body, mind and emotions. She became so good at it that she was able to find employment in a chiropractor's office, which is fairly difficult in this field. In spite of her obvious mastery and a natural talent, Elaine found it impossible to make her living as a Breema practitioner. Instead, she capitalized on her fluency in three languages and became the owner of a small interpreting agency, a business that now pays her bills. She still enjoys working part-time doing Breema, but most of her income comes from interpreting. Elaine is qualified as an interpreter, but not exceptional. There are thousands of interpreters with equal or greater competence, yet they make far less money. Breema is Elaine's life calling, but interpreting is her *Midas Touch*.

Uniqueness

The *Midas Touch* is unique for each of us. You cannot find your financial freedom by practicing anyone else's *Midas Touch*. Unfortunately, most systems of prosperity available today can only teach you how to find the *Midas Touch* of their founders. *Like most of financially successful people, you must throw away all other people's formulas for success and discover your own.* Likewise, your own formula of success, no matter how well it may work for you, will be useless for most of the human race, except for a very few, whose innate *Midas Touch* may be similar to yours.

Vast Field of Possibilities

There is a vast field of possibilities where your *Midas Touch* can be found:

- various careers and businesses (full or part-time), consulting, solo enterprises, partnerships or corporations;
- hobbies, like attending garage sales, sports, writing, astrology or cooking;
- accumulation of objects of values: art, stamps, antiques, memorabilia or oriental carpets;
- production or restoration of objects of value, such as visual arts, pottery, antiques, sculpture or furniture;
- home based businesses, real estate, apartment management child care, or selling your real estate and relocating abroad;
- investment, stock trading or gambling;
- finding a rich partner, providing personal services to the rich, living lavishly on resorts or aboard cruise ships;
- intuition, astrology, prayer, visualization or the occult; or also
- almost anything else you can imagine.

The list is endless. Please note however that your innate *Midas Touch* comes from one or two specific innate abilities of yours and usually can be found only in one, rarely in two or three, of the fields mentioned above. It cannot be found in all of them, or even in many of them.

Political and Socio-Economic Limitations

Like all individuals with a dose of healthy narcissism, I would like to immortalize myself by creating a complete and practical manual of prosperity that would be applicable for all people from all places at all times. Unfortunately, this cannot be done. Therefore, I have to admit that the concept of the *Midas Touch*, discussed in this book, will apply mostly to the inhabitants of prosperous and relatively democratic countries. The place of your birth, as well as your social class, age, gender and race, can put significant limitations on your ability to discover and practice your *Midas Touch*.

Suppose a poor woman from a remote mountain village in Afghanistan was born with a *Midas Touch* in education or politics. For her, such *Midas Touch* was useless under the Taliban, as it is probably still useless now. Only if her country's socio-economic conditions drastically change or if this woman were able to miraculously escape to the U.S., or at least to India, could she hope to achieve prosperity through education or politics.

Central Asia is not the only place that sets limitations on one's ability to use his or her *Midas Touch*. Even in our bastion of democracy, the U.S., there is still a sizable minority of the very poor and uneducated, who may experience almost as many limitations in using their innate *Midas Touch* as our Afghani woman. A drastic change in their socio-economic environment has to occur before some of the deprived, oppressed and prosecuted here and everywhere can apply the book's ideas.

Indeed, our Afghani woman cannot use her *Midas Touch* in politics and education to improve her conditions. However, most of her sisters, cousins, friends and neighbors—equally poor, uneducated and oppressed—may possess a *Midas Touch* in art, sales, marketing or real estate, or in almost anything else. Such individuals, and they would be the majority among the disadvantaged in the U.S. and abroad, would still be able to significantly improve their lives using their *Midas Touch*. For many of them, the *Midas Touch* would still be the path of least resistance out of poverty and deprivation. Therefore, in the vast majority of cases, regardless of your socio-economic conditions, you can drastically improve your living conditions with the *Midas Touch,* as illustrated in the following case.

Case study: Joseph of the Old Testament

According to the Bible, Joseph, son of Jacob, was sold into slavery by his brothers. After various adventures, Joseph found himself in an Egyptian prison, from which he was released due to his skills in dream interpretation. After his release, Joseph became the Pharaoh's advisor, the post he kept until his death. Apparently, Joseph's *Midas Touch* was his natural gift of dream interpretation, which was mainly responsible for his success.

I have no scientific proofs that the Biblical Joseph ever existed. However, his story is a parable for millions of people throughout history, who were able to use their natural gifts to rise from the most difficult socio-economic conditions and reach their ultimate prosperity.

A Formula of Transformation

Occasionally, your *Midas Touch* coincides with your present career, but I have found this rarely to be the case. However, you might be able to modify your present career to integrate your Midas Touch into it, as Mira did.

Case Study: Mira

Mira was a licensed psychotherapist in a solo private practice. Though she was kind, compassionate and qualified, and has truly helped most of her numerous clients to improve their lives, she has not achieved the same success financially. The reason for this was her inability to exchange her kindness and compassion for money, and thus she provided most of her services almost for free. Mira found a solution to this problem in turning her solo practice into a business enterprise. Since she could not make a living by directly engaging her considerable talent for psychotherapy, she began to utilize her *Midas Touch*, which she discovered to be her social connections and organizational ability. Through her friends, she obtained numerous referrals from various state agencies, and became a mental health care provider for most of the health insurance agencies in her state. The fees paid by these agencies were substandard, well below the market rate. Nevertheless, the volume was large enough for Mira to hire a secretary and half-a-dozen interns willing to work for modest wages to gain supervised experience. Now Mira is able to practice her talent helping people, no longer concerned with collecting fees. Her secretary is responsible for it now. Mira dedicates a portion of her day to maintaining relationships with her referral sources and managing her interns to insure her continuous financial success, and the remainder of her time she spends in direct contact with clients.

Mira's case illustrates how in some instances your innate *Midas Touch* can be incorporated into your current occupation. The left and middle portions of the diagram in Fig. 5 show Mira's business as a sole proprietor, and the right portion shows her financial success as the owner of a small corporation, in which she is able to apply her Midas Touch.

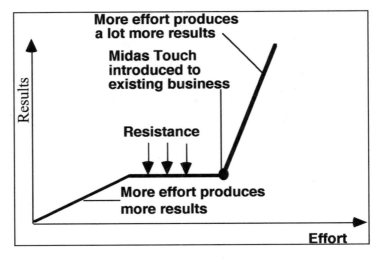

Fig. 5

You may find it impossible to follow Mira's example in incorporating your *Midas Touch* into your own existing business or career. Instead, you may choose to practice your *Midas Touch* and include in it some elements of your present career, as happened with Michael.

Case study: Michael

Michael, originally a teacher and writer, owns one of the largest singles organizations in America. In addition to organizing dances and social events to help singles meet each other, he also organizes educational programs for them. The leading authorities on subjects such as relationships, self-esteem, dating and sexuality give lectures for his organization. Frequently, Michael exercises his own ability as a teacher by lecturing at his own events. He has published a few books on the subject of relationship that he sells at his singles events. As a result, Michael's business rewards him with sizable profits.

Thus Michael was able to combine his talent in teaching

and writing with his personal interest in relationships and with his *Midas Touch* in organization and marketing. And so can you. So let us begin an encounter with "beginner's luck" that runs forever!

CHAPTER FOUR

Do What You Love—But Will the Money Follow?

This chapter is for those who believe that they have a life mission, and also for those who seek to express their highest creative potential on the path to ultimate fulfillment.

If you belong to the majority of my readers, primarily interested in prosperity, unwilling to face all the enormous challenges that any life mission leading to greatness will inevitably involve, then you do not have to read this chapter—unless you are philosophically inclined and want to know what you are missing.

Will the Money Really Follow?

Do What You Love, the Money Will Follow is the title of Marsha Sinetar's bestseller. Her main concept expressed in the title is very appealing. However, already on the first pages of her very inspiring book, Marsha admits that if you do what you love, the money may follow only after a long period of struggle and deprivation. In some instances, Marsha Sinetar acknowledges, even if you do what you love, money will never follow. Unfortunately, Marsha's *Do What You Love* principle did not work for me. Nor did it work for most of my clients, students, teachers and associates.

Eventually, I discovered in history books that many world-renown geniuses frequently could not generate sufficient income by doing what they loved. The list of these geniuses include

Albert Einstein, Wolfang Amadeus Mozart, William Shakespeare and Abraham Lincoln.

The reason that *Do What You Love, the Money Will Follow* does not work for most people is that for the majority of us the *Midas Touch* has no correlation to our greatest talents. If you belong to this sizable majority, your talents will not put bread on the table, and you may have to do something unrelated to what you are best at.

However, a few blessed individuals do what they love, and for them, the money does follow, and a lot of it. Their *Midas Touch* and their greatest creative talents coincide. Even though such individuals are only a small minority, you can still find an endless list of them, including King Solomon, Alexander the Great, Alexander Dumas, Honore de Balsac, Beethoven, Victor Hugo, Walter Scott and Jack London.

Nevertheless, this list does not include such incredible individuals as the Prophet Mohammed, Buddha, Jesus, Mozart and Van Gogh, who did not get paid for doing what they did best and had to rely on other sources of income.

Do What You Love, the Money Will Follow may still work for a few exceptional individuals, who would follow their dreams regardless of financial rewards. Lack of money cannot stop them, poverty does not frighten them, and even half starved, they still manifest their highest potential in creating masterpieces that humanity may recognize only after their death. How can they do this, and is it really worth it? To answer these questions, I have written a book, *Discover and Live Your Destiny*, which will be published in 2005. Here is some of its content relevant to our current discussion on money.

Destiny

We all are born with enormous creative potential. This potential is unique for each of us and is predetermined from birth. Under normal circumstances, your potential is dormant.

Its rare manifestations are usually very brief. The only way to awaken and manifest this potential is by *living your destiny*, which is a life path that allows you to express your innate talents fully. By living your destiny you accomplish your unique mission in life.

Gifts of Destiny

The price of living your Destiny is high: superhuman efforts, huge risk and, frequently, deprivation. What then makes people like Mozart, Van Gogh, Karl Marx, Vladimir Lenin and Che Guevara choose destiny with all its monumental problems that may also include poverty? The rewards of destiny are enormous: a life of purpose, personal freedom and sense of fulfillment. Living your destiny just feels good. Sometimes very good, even euphoric. Problems and obstacles, even disasters, are perceived as opportunities. Moral dilemmas do not linger. They get resolved through actions. Astounding life transformations take place rapidly. And these transformations are usually positive and irreversible.

Destiny and Money

The relationship between destiny and money is illustrated in *Star Wars* through its main character, Luke Skywalker. In the films, he volunteers for the most dangerous missions, risking his life daily. Young Skywalker has no need for recognition. Concerns about financial rewards do not even enter his mind. Luke does not receive any salary for risking his life. Nevertheless, he is never without food, clothing or shelter. The best training, the fastest transportation and the most advance medical care in the galaxy are available to him free of charge. All his expenses are paid by the Rebel Alliance, New Republic, or Princess Leia.

A few daring souls may choose to follow Luke Skywalker and live their destiny like him, disregarding all financial concerns. For them, destiny will become a reward in itself. However, since destiny rarely produces substantial financial gains, you may have to rely on other sources of income, outside of your chosen life path. High expectations of recognition or money may significantly slow your progress on the path of destiny. Life will always provide you with what you need to accomplish your mission, which always includes bare necessities, but rarely luxuries or comfort.

Occasionally, the Money Will Follow

Case study: Vivekananda

Vivekananda was a young East Indian swami (teacher) who decided to present the spiritual teaching of his guru, Ramakrishna, to the West. He started his mission aboard the ship, traveling to the United States to participate in the first Congress of World Religions. No one invited Vivekananda to this Congress, but this did not concern him. He was convinced that, once in the U.S., he would find a way. Aboard the ship, our young swami had very little money left. Most of his savings were spent on his ticket, and the rest got stolen. The loss of all his money, while traveling alone to a strange country where he had no place to stay and no one to ask for help—all this did not bother him a bit. He had faith in his destiny, and it rewarded Vivekananda way beyond his expectations. The rest of his story was like a fairy tale. Aboard the ship, he made friends with some passengers, who helped him financially. Through them, he found food and shelter in the U.S. His new friends devised a way to get him accepted as a presenter at the Congress of World Religions. There, our young swami's speech made a very strong impression on the participants. Worldwide recognition as a prominent philosopher happened almost overnight. Sponsors appeared, who organized his lecture tours. Books got published. A prominent French writer, Roman Rolan, wrote his autobiography with commentary on his teaching, placing him next to Tolstoy and Michaelangelo. The Vedanta Society, which he founded, still functions today, with its several ashrams well attended. Vivekananda asked for nothing and got everything he needed to fulfill his destiny.

The case of Vivekananda illustrates an uncommon occurrence on the path of destiny, when a person does what he or she loves and money soon follows. Such cases, rare as they are, do not only include Indian swamis, but also ordinary people as you and I, as illustrated in the case below.

Case study: Laura

Laura quit her job as a social worker and began pursuing her life passion by started her own catering business in her garage. Soon, recognition and money followed. In three years, she had five hundred employees running several events daily. Laura is very busy, rarely sleeping more than four hours a day. She personally organizes and runs most of her events and thoroughly enjoys the life of a celebrity.

The Money May Never Follow

Vivekananda's and Laura's success in combining destiny and money is a rare exception rather than the rule. The case of Mozart below is a better example of what commonly happens to people of destiny, except that most of them never achieve Mozart's fame even after they die.

Case study: Wolfang Amadeus Mozart

Mozart became one of the most popular composers of all times, but only after his death. He did not receive much recognition when he was alive, struggling to make ends meet most of his life. As is depicted in the film *Amadeus,* Mozart's incredible talent did not pay his bills. In spite of his financial problems, or perhaps because of them, Mozart was able to express his talent fully. Who knows what would have happened if he were recognized in his time? Would he have created more of his masterpieces? Or spoiled by fame, would he have create nothing of lasting value, having been immediately forgotten after his death?

Mozart's case reflects the unfortunate truth: *If you want to live your destiny, and at the same time have luxury and comfort, then destiny may not be enough for you.* Paraphrasing Marsha Sinetar, *do what you love, but discover your Midas Touch and use it to make the money follow.* How this can be done is discussed in the following chapters.

Part II

THE MIDAS TOUCH IN THE FAMILY

CHAPTER FIVE

It's All in the Family

In most instances, your life coping strategies are derived from your family of origin. These strategies can be so ingrained in your subconscious that they can influence, and even determine, your own financial successes and failures.

If your family was good with money, it would be great to discover and use the financial strategies that have been hopefully passed on to you. Hopefully, they are still hidden inside your subconscious waiting to be used. If your family was a financial failure, you may have to erase your family's dysfunctional financial strategies from your mind, or at least avoid implementing them in your own life. In both instances, it will be useful to find out how the transmission of functional and dysfunctional financial strategies takes place.

The Brain Is a Computer

The fatalistic model presented below is, of course, a vast generalization, and is at least partially wrong in many cases. Nevertheless, it does accurately capture the essence of how various life coping skills are transmitted from one generation to another.

According to this model, the brain functions like a computer with most of its software pre-installed. Early childhood experiences mold this original software into fixed patterns that govern your life. Thus, your parents together with your siblings and teachers—external forces over which you had no control—programmed your brain. All the components of your personality, including your behaviors, emotional responses and thought patterns, are established by the age of eight, and very little of it can be radically changed later on. This programming directs your life, making your reactions to events quite predictable.

The Mind Is Not a Computer

I have never come across any adequate scientific or metaphysical explanation of what the mind is and where it is located. For all practical reason, I will presume, hoping that you will agree with me, that the mind either exists outside the brain, or it is part of the brain that contains individuality and free will. Either way, the mind is *not* a computer, but rather something that operates the brain-computer, and therefore is fully capable of making its own decisions, even if such decisions go against the brain's original programming. This explains the fact that no child becomes just the sum of the parents divided by two, and that even identical twins, living in exactly the same conditions, may look identical, but still have distinct, and frequently very different, personalities.

Even though we do possess free will, the influence of parental conditioning is enormous. The *family transmission process*, discussed below, can significantly influence our lives, frequently determining our financial successes and failures.

The Family Transmission Process

So, your family of origin was the original programmer of your brain-computer, just as your parents' brains were programmed by their family of origin, and so on for generations. This explains the *transgenerational transmission process,* the term used by psychologists and family therapists to describe the phenomenon of the transmission of various family traits across generations. The understanding of this *transgenerational transmission process* in your family of origin is crucial in the discovery of your *Midas Touch*. For the sake of simplicity, I will call this process the *family transmission process*. I have found the latter term easier to understand and remember for most of my readers.

In this *family transmission process*, members of the same family from different generations share both their genes and their early childhood programming. As a result, certain family patterns, such as talents and strengths, predisposition to certain illnesses, psychological issues, etc., often persevere through generations. Two case studies below will illustrate how the *family transmission process* operates.

Case study: Alexander the Great

Alexander's father, King Philip of Macedonia, was a competent ruler and one of the most successful military commanders of antiquity, surpassed only by his son and by Julius Caesar.

In spite, or perhaps because, of his obvious abilities in statesmanship, which he transferred to his son via the *family transmission process*, Philip was a heavy drinker. He was also a womanizer. In addition to Olympias, his queen, he also married half-a-dozen junior wives, and was unfaithful to them all with concubines of both genders. For this, Olympias hated Philip and did her best to foster animosity between Alexander and his father. For the most part, she succeeded.

Following the initial infatuation that led to their marriage, the relationship between Alexander's parents grew from bad to worse. Eventually, Philip married another woman, twenty years his junior, with whom he had a son. As a result, Olympias' younger rival replaced her as Philip's queen, and her newborn son became the main contender as Philip's successor. Full of spite, Olympias left Philip and returned to Albania, the country of her origin. She would come back to Macedonia only after Philip's death.

In spite of all his limitations, Philip tried to be a good

father. He cared for Alexander and did not spare any expense to provide his son with an excellent education. Yet, Alexander was not grateful. To the contrary, Philip's achievements brought him envy and discontent. Alexander always attempted to compete with his father. This competition continued even after Philip's death.

Philip fell victim to a blood feud, killed by a captain of his guard. After his death, Alexander's mother murdered her rival, Philip's young queen who had replaced her. She also murdered the woman and Philip's son.

To call this family dysfunctional would be a gross understatement. However, in spite of growing up in such a family, or perhaps because of it, Alexander, the Macedonian, became Alexander the Great, one of the greatest military geniuses of all times. He also became a benevolent and just king of a vast multinational Persian Empire. Alexander was one of the few rulers of antiquity who showed respect and mercy to the people who he had conquered.

Curiously, in spite of all his achievements in the art of military strategy, leadership and diplomacy, *Alexander was unable to overcome the dysfunctional patterns of his family*. Like his father, he was a heavy drinker. Like his father, Alexander also had two chief wives. First, he married Roxane, who proved to be as feisty and treacherous as his mother. A few years later, he took a second wife, the Persian Princess Barsani. Both wives were pregnant by Alexander at the time of his unexpected death. (Some historians believe that Alexander was murdered like his father.) Soon after Alexander's burial, Roxane re-enacted the family tragedy. She followed Alexander's mother example by murdering Barsani. Roxane also murdered and Barsani's and Alexander's son.

In Persia, as well as in Macedonia, murders of dynastic succession were common among the power-hungry royalty, but such murders were usually committed by men. Woman were oppressed and kept far away from politics. Olympias' and Roxane's murderous behaviors were extremely rare. And what about the fact that in both instances, the first wife killed the second wife and the second wife's child to insure her own son's succession to the throne? The statistical probability of all this occurring in the same family is probably close to zero. Yet, if Alexander paid attention to his *family transmission process*, he would probably have noticed the striking similarity between his mother and his first wife. This could have prevented the double murder committed by his mother being re-enacted by his first wife.

Unfortunately, Alexander's family misfortunes did not end with Alexander's and Barsani's deaths. Alexander's mother, his remaining wife, Roxane, and her son, all three were murdered by Alexander's rival.

Case study: Ramona's family

Born in the U.S., Ramona grew up in Paris and spent her adult life in South America, frequently traveling to the U.S. and Europe in connection to her business. Her linguistic abilities—Ramona was fluent in three languages—and her desire to travel seem to have come from her family of origin. Her father, born to a family of merchants involved in international trade for many generations, spoke several language and frequently traveled in relationship to his business.

Ramona's ex-husband, Arthur, also passionately loved to travel. Born in Germany to a family of wealthy merchants like Ramona's, he lived in eight countries, got to visit thirty more, and was a citizen of four. The winds of World War II brought him to South America, where he married Ramona. Their marriage lasted only four years. After their divorce, Arthur moved to England and disappeared without a trace, leaving two infant daughters behind, who had barely known their father.

Following the divorce, Ramona stopped traveling and settled down in one place. For about thirty years, she lived in one city taking care of her daughters, Sylvia and Maria. Even though their father was far away and their mother had stopped traveling, the girls nevertheless caught their parents' itch to travel.

Sylvia started her career as a flight attendant at the age of seventeen and has already visited half of the globe. She speaks four languages fluently—more than her mother, who speaks only three, but less than her father, who speaks six.

Maria has resided in four countries on three continents and became a citizen of two. She is fluent in three languages and works as an interpreter.

The entire story of this family would require volumes. In the end, a strange set of events brought all four of them to live in San Francisco, the place of Ramona's birth.

Thus, the *family transmission process* carried a combination of personality traits as well as a lifestyle related to traveling and relocation across continents, from Ramona's and her husband's ancestors to Sylvia and Maria. Each member of Ramona's family generated his or her income—which was quite substantial for some of them at times—either through language skills or through international travel and trade.

* * *

This almighty *family transmission process* determines your predisposition to a great many things, including your financial success in certain fields, as well as your failure in others.

External circumstances, as well as your own effort, may significantly modify your family of origin's influence in your present life. Psychology, religion and spirituality, as discussed in Chapters Fifteen, Nineteen, Twenty and Twenty-One, have helped millions to modify, and at times even erase, some of their parental conditioning.

However, we have to apply the reality principle here. Contrary to the claims of some lecturers on human potential and popular psychology, as well as some authors of self-help books, the influence of your family of origin on your life can never be entirely eradicated. In my thirty-five years of experience in self-help and twenty years of education and experience in psychotherapy, I have never seen a single individual able to get rid of early childhood conditioning entirely. I have observed hundreds of people, including myself, who managed to significantly modify and improve the early childhood programming installed in our brain-computer. Many of us have been able to delete whole sections of parental conditioning responsible for our dysfunctions, but never to eradicate this conditioning altogether.

I can testify that psychotherapy, self-help, religion, the occult and a few other methodologies can and do help. In a few instances, rapid positive changes, even an instantaneous transformation, can occur. However, such cases are exceptional. For most of us overcoming parental conditioning will require time and effort, and frequently a lot of money.

"It Is Useless to Resist, My Son"

Such was Darth Vader's propaganda in the *Return of the Jedi*. In case you do not know, Darth Vader is one of the main characters of *Star Wars*. In the above statement, he refers to the futility of resisting ultimate evil, personified in this film by the Emperor. Darth Vader's son, Luke Skywalker, did not heed his father's advice. He challenged the power of evil and overcame it, while resolving his family of origin issues in the process. The story of Luke Skywalker is a symbolic representation of what it truly takes to resolve such issues. It usually requires tremendous effort to overcome the negative programming and cultural delusions deeply imbedded in our subconscious by our family of origin. This is a noble task for a few heroic souls, but most of us are not willing or even capable of such enormous efforts and ultimate sacrifices.

The good news is that psychological health, if such a thing exists, is not necessary for financial success. *We all can become prosperous in spite of the fact that we may be imperfect, full of issues, with our brains programmed by our dysfunctional families of origin.*

Suppose your family was as bad as that of Alexander the Great. Maybe it was even worse. Still, your struggle to survive in such a dysfunctional family with inadequate, or even malicious or psychotic parents, does not necessarily doom you to financial failure. Growing up in an atmosphere of deprivation and persecution or in the midst of social unrest and mortal danger does not always destroy or diminish you either. On the contrary, *some of us who have endured harsh conditions in early childhood have developed exceptional strength of character as well as exceptional abilities.*

It is not only your family's greatness, hopefully already transferred to you, but also your family's "badness" that determines your *Midas Touch.* Yes, paradoxical as it may seem, your family's dysfunctions, transferred to you from your ancestors, at times may become the foundation of your success.

In my professional experience as a psychotherapist, I have never encountered any defect of character that was not the flip side of a great talent. All the qualities which you despise in yourself or in others may manifest as talents and strengths under different circumstances. On the road to prosperity, the qualities of character which you may consider to be your defects may become your most powerful assets.

The Midas Touch and Psychological Issues

Do you have to struggle with your family of origin issues to achieve prosperity? It is too early to say for sure at this point, but most likely you do not have to.

There is a very high probability that you already possess a few excellent financial strategies passed on to you via the *family transmission process,* and you do not have to change any of your early childhood conditioning, dysfunctional as it may appear, to use these strategies in your life. Resolving your family of origin issues will surely improve your psychological health. In most instances however, this will not significantly alter your income.

There is still a sizable minority for whom the above rule does not apply. For them, the struggle with early childhood negative programming is unavoidable on the journey to prosperity. Such cases will be discussed in Chapter Fifteen.

Family of Origin and the Midas Touch

My observations of hundreds of my clients, students, friends and associates indicate that there is a significant correlation between one's *Midas Touch* and one's family financial history. Frequently, all you have to do to discover your *Midas Touch* is to analyze the successful and unsuccessful financial strategies used by your parents, your parents' siblings, your grandparents and their siblings, as well as your own siblings. What worked for them financially is also likely to work for you.

While there is a close correlation between one's *Midas Touch* and one's family of origin financial successes and failures, cases of a totally identical *Midas Touch,* shared by all family members through generations, are very rare. Due to ever changing life circumstances, your *Midas Touch* is likely to be similar to that of your parents and siblings, but rarely identical.

It is also possible that your *Midas Touch* may have nothing to do with your family of origin, and you will have to apply other methodologies presented in this book to discover it. The latter is especially true if your family of origin has experienced financial failures for many generations. We all, including your parents and grandparents, are born with a *Midas Touch*. The major reason your parents or grandparents may have been poor, working hard and never making enough money, may be that they could not discover or apply their *Midas Touch* due to the socio-economic conditions of their times. Even in this case, you can still benefit from looking at their dysfunctional financial strategies to avoid repeating them.

Counter-suggestibility

Some of you may ask, "My parents are financially successful. Why then am I such a failure?"

A small percentage of us, including the author of this book, are counter-suggestible. These counter-suggestible individuals have a strong tendency to resist all external influences. Many creative thinkers and revolutionaries succeeded precisely because they were counter-suggestible. From childhood on they did not conform to the norms, but felt compelled to do the opposite, or at least to act differently from what they were told to do by their parents and teachers.

If you indeed are counter-suggestible, you may be compelled to rebel against your family. Therefore, you might be unconsciously rejecting your family's functional financial strategies, but accepting those that do not work.

If your family was a total financial failure, your counter-suggestibility becomes a valuable asset, making it easier to avoid your family's dysfunctional patterns.

Having Darth Vader for a Parent

"What do I do if I do not like my parents?" you may wonder. The answer to this and all other important questions can be found in *Star Wars*. (I am joking of course.) Luke Skywalker, a symbolic representation of an unpretentious American genius, hated his father, called Darth Vader in the film. Three times, father and son were close to killing each other. At the end, Luke finally succeeded in cutting off Darth Vader's hand.

In spite of such animosity, Luke does not hesitate to use the multiplicity of talents and abilities that he inherited from his father. This illustrates that you do not have to like your parents to use a *Midas Touch* received from them. Besides, there is always an Anakin Skywalker within every Darth Vader. (Hopefully, you remember that Anakin Skywalker was Darth Vader's name before he turned bad.)

"What do I do if it is painful for me even to think about my parents?" you may also ask. In such extreme cases, you do not have to suffer. Simply skip Chapter Seven, perhaps even Chapters Six, Eight and Nine, all dealing with the family of origin. You will still have plenty of opportunities to discover your *Midas Touch* in other chapters.

CHAPTER SIX

Your Grandparents

Worksheets

This and most of the following chapters contain various worksheets that will encourage you to make written statements, responding to the book's queries. By making and examining these statements, it will become clear to you that your life's events are not random, but form distinct patterns, and studying these patterns will lead you to discover your *Midas Touch*.

You will not be able to fill in the blank spaces of all the worksheets. Some of them won't apply to you, so just leave them blank. Keep in mind that there are no right or wrong statements, no passing or failing, and that your own interpretation of your life events, as well as of your family history, is the only valid one.

Please do not rely on your memory alone. Write your statements down, using the blank spaces provided. This will prevent your unconscious resistances from playing tricks on you. Besides, you will need your statements in a written form for the final chapters of this book.

The process presented here rarely fails. Hundreds of my students have tried it before you and succeeded in discovering their *Midas Touch,* as will you.

Your Grandparents

As we discussed in the previous chapter, the almighty *family transmission process* may be responsible for your financial successes and failures, and by studying your family of origin financial patterns, you are likely to discover your *Midas Touch*. Examining such patterns will also help you to detect your family's faulty financial strategies that you may have been unconsciously applying in your own life. This detective work will not take much effort and can produce remarkable results.

Very few people can trace their family history beyond their grandparents. A thorough research a few hundred years back may bear interesting results. For most of us however, such research will be time-consuming and the results will be unreliable. Why conduct genealogical research for months or years, if you can discover your *Midas Touch* in a few days, sometimes even in a few hours? If you know nothing about your grandparents' financial strategies and have no easy way to find out, you can skip the next two sections altogether.

Successful Financial Strategies

In the blank spaces below, make a list of your grandparents' successful financial strategies, such as jobs, businesses, investment, etc. It would be useful and fun to enhance your knowledge of the subject by talking to your parents about it, provided they are willing and available. Here, as well as in other worksheets, there is no specific formula for filling in the blanks, as long as you write what makes sense to you.

_____

_____

_____

_____

_____

_____

Faulty Financial Strategies

In the blank spaces below, write down a list of your grandparents' faulty financial strategies. Occupations or business in which your grandparents worked hard for minimal wages should also be included here. Include losses due to poor investment, theft, lawsuits, sibling rivalry, wars, revolutions, civil unrest, economic volatility, natural disasters, failed businesses or any other reason. This can help you avoid following the patterns of financial losses that may have plagued your family for generations.

_____
_____
_____
_____
_____
_____
_____
_____
_____
_____

The Midas Touch Overlooked

Like many of my students, you may have found that your grandparents worked hard for a living, never quite making enough to get ahead. You might have drawn the conclusion that following their footsteps will not lead to riches. Such a conclusion may be at least partially wrong. You may have overlooked at least one of the following:

Marriage. It is likely that one, perhaps both of your grandmothers, were not gainfully employed, staying home to raise children. Even though your grandfathers may not have provided a lavish lifestyle for them, still there may be a pattern in your family of one marriage partner financially supporting another.

Here, you have to consider that before World War II a large percentage of women did not work outside the house. Among the privileged, most women did not work at all. Therefore, you cannot conclude that marrying into riches is your *Midas Touch* based on observing your grandparents alone. However, if you can also observe this pattern in the lives of your parents, of your parents' siblings and your own siblings, then there is a significant possibility that finding a marriage partner who will provide for you is your *Midas Touch*.

Marrying into riches may present a moral dilemma to you. I will discuss the solutions to moral dilemmas in the next chapter. Here, it is sufficient to say that any financial strategy presents moral issues. If living with a rich partner is your *Midas Touch*, then the moral dilemmas associated with it would be easier to sort out than the ones you may be struggling with at your present job.

Keep it in mind that a *Midas Touch* is rarely, if ever, gender specific. If you are a male, and your grandmothers and you mother were well provided for, there is a good chance that you can apply their financial strategy in your own life. Such a strategy may include gender role reversal. *Beware though that domestic responsibilities can sometimes be much greater than at any job.*

Investment. Your grandparents may have invested a small portion of their hard earned money in stocks, and these stocks may have gone up sky-high over the years. The profit that your grandparents may have made in stocks was probably very small compared with their wages. Nevertheless, there is a considerable possibility that your grandparents could have made a lot more money in stocks, if they had put more effort in it. Even a single occurrence of a handsome profit may indicate a *Midas Touch*. A double occurrence of such a profit through the same activity hints a high probability of it, and a multiple occurrence suggests almost a certainty.

Real estate. Your grandparents may have worked hard for meager wages, but they were still able to buy their own house, and its market value increased over the years. This is an indication that your grandparents may have had their *Midas Touch* in real estate, and possibly transferred it to you through the *family transmission process.*

Please note that almost everyone who bought real estate after World War II enjoyed a huge equity increase over the years. There is no guarantee that this real estate boom will continue forever, and there are many indications that it will not. If investing in real estate was indeed your grandparents' *Midas Touch,* than the increase in their real estate value would have been considerably greater than the national average for the same period, both adjusted to inflation.

Inheritance. One of your grandparents may have inherited money, business, land, valuables, real estate, etc. Even if such an inheritance was small, it may still indicate a *Midas Touch* in the area of inheritance. If more than one of your grandparents inherited, and/or at least one of your parents inherited as well, there is a significant possibility that you will also inherit. Therefore, you may consider establishing good relationships with the person that you may inherit from. This may naturally produce moral dilemmas, which are discussed at the end of the next chapter.

Social connections. At the time of your grandparents, advertising and marketing were not as sophisticated as now, and most business deals were made through social connections, especially with small business owners. In many instances, social connections would determine one's chances for employment and promotion. This is still true today. If your grandparents were able to utilize their social connections for promoting their businesses, or getting their jobs and promotions, perhaps you can also do the same. Then, using your social connections for profit or professional advancement is your *Midas Touch*. Such a realization may open a Pandora's box of moral dilemmas, which will be also dealt with later on.

The areas of human experience mentioned above are not the only ones where your grandparents could have been financially successful. Your grandparents could also have manifested their *Midas Touch* in numerous other areas, related or unrelated to their jobs or businesses. So, list all such areas of their financial success, which you may have previously overlooked, below.

_____

_____

_____

_____

_____

_____

_____

_____

Grandparents' Siblings

Very few people know much about their grandparents' siblings. So, if you have no idea how they were making a living and no convenient way to get this information, skip the two following sections altogether. However, if you are able to analyze the financial strategies of your grandparents' brothers and sisters, it can help you to discover your own *Midas Touch*.

Successful Financial Strategies

In the blank spaces below, write down a list of the successful financial strategies utilized by your grandparents' siblings. Ask your parents about their uncles and aunts, if you can.

Do not forget that the *Midas Touch* is rarely a career. Instead, it can be found in financially successful marriages, investment, real estate, social connections and almost anything else.

_____
_____
_____
_____
_____
_____
_____
_____
_____

Faulty Financial Strategies

In the blank spaces below, write down a list of the faulty financial strategies of your grandparents' brothers and sisters. List below the occupations or business in which they worked hard for minimal wages, as well as their losses due to poor investment, theft, lawsuits, sibling rivalry, wars, revolutions, civil unrest, economic volatility, natural disasters, failed businesses or any other reason.

_____
_____
_____
_____
_____
_____
_____
_____
_____

Hopefully, you have already found a few clues that point to your own financial strategies. However, your real discoveries will begin in the next chapter, where we will discuss the financial strategies of your parents.

CHAPTER SEVEN

Your Parents

Blame It All on Your Parents

No one ever had a greater influence on your character formation than your parents. They may have passed on to you their family of origin financial strategies that were passed to them by their parents. Most probably, you are still unconsciously applying these family strategies that are responsible for your successes or failures. Indeed, many of those who have achieved prosperity have applied the successful financial strategies of their parents, while avoiding the strategies that led their parents to financial disasters. So, let's examine your parents' financial successes and failures which may help you to discover your own *Midas Touch*.

Note: Talking about parents frequently produces strong emotional responses in some of us, compelling us to blame our parents for everything that goes wrong in our life. When you get to this chapter's worksheets you may find yourself describing how terrible your parents are, filling in the blanks with various adjectives reflecting their qualities of character. Stop! Processing your feelings about your parents may be useful, but will not help in discovering your *Midas Touch*. Therefore, if you must deal with your childhood issues, do it as a separate project, following the guidelines in Chapter Fifteen.

Successful Financial Strategies

In the blank spaces below, write down a list of your parents' successful financial strategies. It would be useful and fun to enhance your knowledge of the subject by talking to your parents about it, provided they are willing and available. Make sure that you do not overlook the instances of their success in investment, gambling, real estate, or anything else, no matter how unusual, bizarre or even illegal it may appear. If your parents were able to produce or accumulate objects of value that went up in price, or utilize their social connections for business or professional advancement, also include this in the list below. If one of your parents was at least partially financially supported by another, include this possibility below as well. Remember that your parents', as well as yours, *Midas Touch* can be almost any human endeavor.

You do not have to describe your parents' character here. So, do not fill the blanks with statements such as: "My mother was good and kind," or "My father was never home." Such statements might be true, but they will not lead you to your *Midas Touch*. Instead, fill in the blanks below with the activities and areas in which your parents were financially successful. If your father was or is a high- ranking officer in the Army for example, fill in the blank with "armed services" or "upper management" or "working for the government" as your possible *Midas Touch*.

Father:

_____

_____

_____

_____

_____

_____

_____

Mother:

_____

_____

_____

_____

_____

_____

_____

_____

_____

_____

_____

Faulty Financial Strategies

In the blank spaces that follow, write down a list of your parents' faulty financial strategies. This would include occupations in which your parents worked hard for low wages or their unprofitable businesses. Also, list your parents' losses due to poor investment, theft, lawsuits, sibling rivalry, wars, revolutions, civil unrest, economic volatility, natural disasters, failed businesses or anything else.

Do not include here statements criticizing your parents, such as, "My parents were a total financial failure," or "My parents were so stingy." Such statements might be true, but they will not lead you to your _Midas Touch_, and will not prevent you from repeating your parents' financial disasters. Instead, state in the blanks below the activities and areas in which your parents failed financially. If your father lost tons of money in gambling, write down "gambling." Or if your mother invested in her brother's business and he cheated her out of her money, write down something like "investing with relatives" or "trusting siblings with money."

Father:

_____
_____
_____
_____
_____
_____
_____
_____
_____
_____

Mother:

_____
_____
_____
_____
_____
_____
_____
_____
_____

Uncles and Aunts

Learning about your uncles' and aunts' financial successes and failures can also be revealing in discovering your own *Midas Touch*. Usually, such information can be easily attained from your parents. However, if you have no convenient way to find out how your uncles and aunts made money, skip the two following sections altogether.

Successful Financial Strategies

In the blank spaces below, write down a list of your uncles' and aunts' successful financial strategies. Do not forget that *a Midas Touch is rarely a career*. Instead, it can be found in financially successful marriages, investment, real estate, social connections, etc.

_____

_____

_____

_____

_____

_____

_____

_____

_____

_____

Faulty Financial Strategies

In the blank spaces below, write down a list of your uncles' and aunts' faulty financial strategies: the occupations or business in which they worked hard for low wages, as well as their losses due to poor investment, theft, lawsuits, sibling rivalry, wars, revolutions, civil unrest, economic volatility, natural disasters, failed businesses or any other reason.

_____

_____

_____

_____

_____

_____

_____

_____

Rebel without a Cause

It is part of human development to rebel against one's parents, which may take the form of rejecting many of their values. Some people attempt to eradicate even the memory of their family of origin altogether, which, of course, cannot be done. No matter how hard you try, some of your parents' qualities will always remain in you. This rebellion may lead some to rejecting the functional financial strategies of their family of origin, while unconsciously applying those that do not work.

Rebel with a Cause

Now, let's reject your family of origin's faulty financial strategies consciously, as illustrated by the following example.

Case study: John

John's grandmother had three brothers who went into business together. The business was successful, until it was discovered that one of the brothers was dishonest. He was stealing from the other two, who eventually suffered substantial losses as a result. This pattern of theft in the family persevered through two generations. Thus, John's aunt, a daughter of the dishonest brother, cheated on her sister and her cousins twice in matters of inheritance. Her nephew, Mark, a grandson of the dishonest brother, offered John a deal that appeared as a great investment opportunity. John, armed with knowledge of the family history, bluntly refused. Mark found other investors and soon prospered. However, years later Mark was caught cheating on his cousin, who was also his best friend and a business partner, thus reenacting this old family pattern again. By rejecting Mark's proposition, John missed an opportunity to make substantial profits, but he also avoided substantial losses from being cheated. In addition, he escaped family quarrels, heartaches and, most probably, a costly litigation.

Following John's example, examine your parents' and their siblings' dysfunctional financial strategies, especially those that resulted in substantial financial losses and list below the strategies that would allow you to avoid such losses.

_____

_____

_____

_____

_____

_____

_____

_____

_____

Unfortunately, financial disasters caused by spouses, siblings, parents, children and other family members are a lot more common that most are willing to admit. Not always are they caused by theft or cheating. Frequently such disasters are the results of honest mistakes, inexperience or incompetence. Regardless of the causes, if you discover such a pattern in your family, consider following John's example and avoid financial involvement with the family members altogether.

Profiting from Crime

What if there is a pattern in your family of making tons of money through crime, such as robbery, piracy, selling drugs or prostitution? Do you have then to get involved in illegal activities, joining the local Mafia perhaps, to discover your *Midas Touch*? No, you do not have to. In most cases, a *Midas Touch* that operated in a criminal activity is transferable to legal businesses as well, as illustrated by the following examples.

Case study: Michael

Michael was born in a poor black neighborhood in Oakland, California. His father and his older brother were involved in drug dealing. This allowed the family to enjoy a fairly comfortable middle class lifestyle, even though they lived in the ghetto, surrounded by poverty. In their criminal circle, both Michael's father and brother were respected as leaders known for their caution, self-control and superior communication skills.

Michael did not follow his family in becoming a drug dealer. Instead, he now owns an employment agency. He is also a motivational speaker and a published author. Michael's skills in taking calculated risks, managing people and persuasive communication are very similar to those that made his father and brother successful in their criminal business. However, he applies such life strategies that he learned from his family in a field far remote from the world of crime where his family achieved their initial success.

Case study: Bertha

A well-known San Francisco psychologist joked, "There are only two human activities where you must pay for love: psychotherapy and prostitution." Bertha, a licensed psychotherapist, would probably agree with this statement. Her grandmother was a prosperous owner of a bordello, with at least a dozen prostitutes working for her. Bertha seems to have inherited her grandmother's *Midas Touch,* but she applies it in a quite different field, far remote from prostitution. Bertha conducts her psychotherapy practice as a business, in many respects similar to her grandmother's. Bertha employs a score of interns working under her license in her psychotherapy office. Bertha herself sees only a few clients. She mostly performs administrative duties, including training her interns and providing them with clients.

Contradictions

At times, the analysis of your family financial strategies may bring contradictory results. It may happen that the grandparents were very successful in conducting their family business, while the parents almost ruined it, and the children now fluctuate between success and failure in the same business. It is also common that one parent (or grandparent) manifested his or her *Midas Touch* in the same activity where another one failed. And occasionally, the same activity may be the cause of both family fortune and family ruin, as illustrated by the following example.

Case study: Julia

Julia, a well-known musician and composer, had most of her money invested in the stock of a particular company connected to her family history. Julia's grandfather bought these shares long time ago. For years, the share price was going up, and the grandfather made a family fortune on his investment. Unfortunately, the stock traders' principle, "Whatever goes up, must come down," was true for Julia's family. During a recession, the value of grandfather's stock went down almost to zero, and the fortune was lost. Nevertheless, the grandfather faithfully held on to his shares and then passed them on to his son, Julia's father. Eventually, the stock made a spectacular return, during which the family made another fortune on it. The father, preoccupied with family business, paid little attention to the stock market. As had happened with the previous stockholder, the grandfather, he did not notice when his shares began to move down again. When he did notice that he had lost a fortune, it was already too late. The share price went down almost to zero again, after many years of spectacular performance. The father held on to his shares, and passed them on to Julia. Julia, dedicated to her career in music, hardly noticed, as

the price of her shares skyrocketed again, significantly outper-
forming the bull market of the 1990s. Like her grandfather
and her father before her, she also failed to notice that the price
of shares began to rapidly drop in the fall of 2000. Only when
she attended my class, *Psychology of Money*, did Julia realize that
investing in this particular stock was both her *Midas Touch* and
a possibility of financial disaster. As a result of this analysis, she
developed a strategy that would allow her to continue making
money in the stock market without losing it all from time to
time. Her strategy lies in the domain of financial consulting
and is beyond the scope of this book. It suffices to say here
that after consulting a professional financial adviser she began
diversifying and also started using stop loss orders. Thus, Julia
managed to apply the family's *Midas Touch,* and at the same
time to avoid her family's dysfunctional financial strategies.

Gender Issues

The *family transmission process* does not respect gender
boundaries. Thus, both males and females with fathers financially
successful in historically male occupations (such as wood cutting,
military, police, etc.) or with mothers in historically female
occupations (such as weaving, child care, nursing, etc.) can succeed in the same field as either parent, regardless of gender.
They can also excel in a similar field more historically typical of
their gender. In most instances, *it was not the field that made
your family fortune, but the strategies that your family applied in
this field.* And such strategies are usually transferable.

What if you are a male, and your mother's *Midas Touch*
was in marrying your father? Hers was a Cinderella story, finding a Prince who provided for her beyond her dreams. Is there
a chance for you to reproduce your mother's success in your
own marriage? The following case may provide an answer.

Case study: Jerry

Jerry, a licensed psychologist, came from a wealthy family. His mother never worked, nor was she burdened with family responsibilities. The most successful financial enterprise in her life was marrying Jerry's father, who was able and willing to provide for her. Jerry shared his mother's ineptitude in business. In spite of his education and experience, he could not generate a sufficient income from his prestigious occupation as a psychologist. However, he also shared his mother's *Midas Touch* in choosing a spouse who provided for him. Jerry's wife does not have his level of education. Hers is a high school diploma, while his is a doctorate and license in psychology, which took him nine years of studies and three years of internship to achieve. Nevertheless, it is her retail business, not Jerry's psychology practice, that generates most of the family income.

* * *

If, in fact, your mother stayed home, supported by your father, this may reflect a possibility that marrying into riches is your *Midas Touch,* regardless of your gender. A possibility, but not a certainty. Here, your mother's financial success may very well be a generational or cultural phenomenon, rather than a personal strategy. Look for additional confirmations of this strategy in other sections of this book.

It is equally possible that your *family transmission process* passed on to you totally different successful financial strategies, rather than this one.

Moral Dilemmas

Many readers, who are not already married or involved in romantic partnerships, want a marriage based on romantic love, rather on financial considerations. In this case consider the following:

It does not appear that poor partners make better spouses than rich partners. However, there is more than enough statistical evidence indicating that financial problems commonly cause divorce. Most likely, you will have as many chances for family problems with a rich partner as with a poor one. With a rich partner however, financial problems are less likely to become as severe. In addition, your chances of finding romantic love with a rich spouse will be about the same as with a poor one. So, with all things being equal, marrying a rich partner does present a few potential advantages.

This family pattern of attracting a prosperous spouse may manifest in your life even when you give no thoughts to it, as is apparent in the case of Jerry, previously discussed above.

Case study: Jerry (continued)

When Jerry courted his wife to be, he had no idea that she would become financially successful. Just the opposite, both he and his bride expected that Jerry would be the main family provider. As we discussed above, the *family transmission process* decided otherwise.

* * *

Do you absolutely refuse to consider looking for a wealthy spouse and prefer to stay with your present romantic partner instead? I understand. If I were you, I would do the same. However, let's consider another possibility discussed below that might be acceptable to you.

The Power Behind the Throne

In our still male-dominated society, we usually credit the males with all achievements, frequently overlooking their wives' contributions to their success. Thus, history books praise one of the greatest Byzantine emperors, Justinian, barely mentioning his wife Theodora, who was probably mainly responsible for his success. Hillary Clinton contributed to her husband's successful presidency at least as much as he did. Nevertheless, he got most of the praise, not her. This phenomenon of women doing the work and men getting the glory is common in all social circles, as discussed below.

Case study: Tatyana

When Tatyana married Andrei, a junior officer in the Soviet Army, she had no financial considerations in mind. She was in love. Besides, she got pregnant. Marriage seemed the most natural continuation of their relationship. Andrei was bright, hard working and dedicated to the cause of communism, but so were thousands of other Soviet Army junior officers. Nevertheless, he became a general, able to provide Tatyana with all the privileges of the Soviet elite. Most of her married life, Tatyana stayed home taking care of their two children, which was extremely rare in the Soviet Union at that time. In the 1960s and 1970s, most of Russian families barely survived on two persons' income. Tatyana's contribution to the family success was not financial. Nevertheless, it was probably as great as her husband's. It was she who advised Andrei in all major decisions and encouraged him to go beyond what he and others considered possible. To put it simply, Tatyana made a general out of a junior lieutenant.

Tatyana's *Midas Touch* was in picking a husband with the potential to succeed on a large scale, when he was still at the very start of his career, and then in supporting and encouraging him to move up the ladder of success. Perhaps her example will encourage you to look for a financially promising spouse, or to support your present partner in manifesting his or her *Midas Touch*. It is a great talent to be able to encourage a spouse in manifesting success in his or her career. It is also a talent for which society gives very little credit. Nevertheless, if you possess such a talent, it may become your *Midas Touch*.

Adoption

I did not accumulate much data on the subject of *Midas Touch* transmission to adopted children. The few of them whom I did observe were as bound by the *family transmission process* of their adoptive families as those raised by their biological parents.

Other Dilemmas

Besides a few of the moral dilemmas discussed above, you may find other significant issues discouraging you from practicing the *Midas Touch* that you may have received from your family of origin. In addition, you may have to face fear, inertia, denial, and other inner and outer resistances that you may have to overcome in any attempt to change your life. Do not despair. The *Midas Touch* is the road of least resistance to financial success. You will still have to overcome some difficulties and solve a few problems, even while practicing your *Midas Touch*. Nevertheless, *a life journey with an engaged Midas Touch will be much easier and present fewer problems and moral dilemmas than the one you are taking now.* Can you honestly say that you have no issues with your bosses, supervisors, co-workers, clients or customers, that you do not struggle at your present job or business, or that you do not have to deal with moral dilemmas now?

* * *

I hope that you have already developed a few interesting ideas about your *Midas Touch* by observing your family's financial successes and failures. The following chapters will help to clarify those ideas.

CHAPTER EIGHT

Your Siblings

Your parents may have passed on their family of origin financial strategies to you and to your siblings. Most probably, your siblings apply these family strategies differently than you do. Therefore, by observing your brothers' and sisters' financial successes and failures, you can discover the best and worst examples of how such strategies may work under present conditions, which may lead you to discovering your own *Midas Touch*.

Note: Even if you do not have siblings, this chapter may still apply to you.

Similarities and Differences

Obviously, your siblings are similar to you in many respects, which may have resulted from the same combination of genes and similar parenting. Yet, you all turned out different; not only in appearance, but also in your life fortunes. You and your siblings may have received the same family strategies via the *family transmission process*. However, *the roles that you played in your family determined how these strategies were developed and how they are applied at present*.

Family Roles

Marriage and family therapists, notably Virginia Satir, have written extensively about the roles people are "assigned" in their family of origin. Below is a summary of contemporary thought on this subject with a few of my own additions:

Depending on their birth order, children are encouraged by the parents and their siblings to play certain roles in the family. Thus, the firstborn usually plays the role of the parents' helper and confidant, especially in single parent homes. Occasionally, the second-born takes this role, depending on the family traditions. Such children are more likely to work in the family business and inherit most of their parents' real estate. The children who follow the first (responsible) child are encouraged or even forced by the family dynamics to play different roles. The most common of these roles include the spoiled brat, the scapegoat, the run-away, the favorite, the peace maker and the entertainer. Once children are assigned these roles, the family dynamic compels them to become experts in playing such roles. Each sibling develops certain qualities of character, as well as talents and abilities, appropriate for the role that he or she plays, while the expression of other talents may be discouraged. When such children become adults, they tend to continue playing these roles all their lives. For example, this is what may happen in a family with four children when they grow up: the "parental" child may remain at home to help in the family business, the favorite may go to college, the rebel may move to the other coast, and the scapegoat may become a financial failure.

Getting Attention

Parental attention is crucial for child development. In many families however, children never get enough of it. As a result, each child develops his or her own way to compete for attention. The most common strategies of getting parental attention are described below. Depending on birth order and family traditions, each sibling *unconsciously* chooses different strategies from the family's repertoire.

Having learned a particular approach to get your parents' attention, you are likely to apply it in all your relationships later on. Thus, *this strategy of getting parental attention in your child-hood may still influence your financial successes and failures now.*

So, let's examine some common strategies that children use to get attention, and see if you can recognize some of them in your own repertoire.

The Sacrificial Lamb

In some families, children are encouraged to sacrifice their needs for the needs of their parents. Such children are frequently, but not always, the firstborn. They do most of the house chores, take care of their younger siblings and start helping out in the family business. This family role may solicit the parents' love and attention. However, such children are frequently taken for granted, and their rewards are rarely proportionate to their effort. In some dysfunctional families, the strategy of self-sacrifice hardly works at all, since the parents remain dissatisfied no matter how much a child tries to please them. Such overly responsible children usually become overly responsible adults, typical "company" men and women, dedicated to their employer's welfare. Unfortunately, a life strategy of self-sacrifice rarely, if ever, becomes a *Midas Touch*.

The Obedient Child

Children who use obedience to get parental attention and approval, while avoiding rejection, follow their parents' instructions to the letter, never voicing any objections. They are rarely encouraged to develop their distinct personalities and frequently are *not* motivated to express any particular talent. They may grow up into passive-aggressive adults with no initiative. This life strategy, especially when applied unconsciously, may become an obstacle to discovering and implementing one's *Midas Touch*.

The Confidant

In many families, especially in single parent households, one of the children may be forced by family dynamics to play the role of the parent's confidant. This child gets the parental love and attention by being a sounding board for the parent. People who learn this strategy in early childhood may become adults with superior counseling skills. However, only in a very few instances does one's *Midas Touch* correlate with one's counseling skills. In most cases, it does not. Unless one is born with a *Midas Touch* in counseling, psychotherapy or related fields, this life strategy may become an obstacle to achieving prosperity.

"Make Me Proud"

Many parents enjoy showing off their children's special talents and abilities. Some of these parents frequently ignore their children's true gifts, and encourage the development only of those talents and skills that can be proudly exhibited to relatives, friends and neighbors. In response to their parents' needs, and driven by their own needs for love and attention, children may develop some of the life strategies discussed below.

The Professor

Very few achievements bring children as much positive reinforcements from parents as straight "A"s at school. These children learn to associate their academic achievement with parental love. Such children usually have at least above average talent in academia, to which they may dedicate their lives in adulthood. In most instances however, education has little correlation with one's *Midas Touch*. Consider the case of Jerry in the previous chapter for example.

The Beauty Queen

Some children get much positive reinforcement from parents by dedicating their lives to their attractive appearance. Such children frequently grow into beautiful adults, who rely on their looks more than on their wits. These people have most to lose when they get older. For some of them, especially women, old age is a real tragedy. Probably, there is some correlation between physical beauty and financial success. In most instances however, even for those who are exceptionally attractive, sexy, well dressed, etc., physical appearance alone cannot guarantee high income. Even if an attractive appearance is your *Midas Touch*, it usually takes a lot more than just good looks to achieve prosperity.

The Clown

Playing the role of clown may have provided a child with parental attention and love. Making parents laugh may have also enabled such a child to escape punishment and diffuse family quarrels. In adulthood however, such strategy can do more harm than good. Unless being a clown is your *Midas Touch*, in entertainment for example, people may not seriously consider you for promotions and lucrative business deals.

The Rebel

Some children get more attention for their "badness" than for their "goodness." For a growing child, even negative attention, including punishment, is better than no attention at all. So, some children are forced by their family system to develop a life strategy of getting attention by misbehaving, talking back, violating rules, etc. In extreme cases, this life strategy may lead to severe drug abuse and a life of crime. In more typical cases, it may lead to rebelling against the successful financial strategies of your family of origin and accepting those that do not work.

There is a good side to this strategy. Children who learn how to rebel may grow up into creative adults able to challenge socially acceptable mediocrity and develop their own ideas. It seems to me that most creative individuals, able to initiate a revolutionary breakthrough in technology or art, played the rebel's role in childhood, at least to some degree. Unfortunately, not every rebellious child grows up into a creative genius.

The Rebel Leader

Occasionally, a child who plays the role of family rebel may evolve into a rebel leader. In additional to getting negative parental attention, a child who plays this role usually gets positive reinforcement from his or her siblings and peers, which makes this strategy especially appealing in adolescence. In extreme cases, such children not only become juvenile delinquents, but also rise to leadership positions in gangs. In most cases however, little rebel leaders grow into adults with superior skills in dealing with the deprived, persecuted, oppressed, different, unpopular and even weird. Unfortunately, such skills frequently go along with poor skills in relating to authority. Unless your *Midas Touch* lies in the area of social work, mediation and other similar fields, the life strategy of a rebel leader may easily become a hindrance to achieving prosperity. Rebel leaders are ideally suited to become political activists and revolutionaries. Such occupations are historically associated with a life of self-sacrifice, personal deprivation and high risk, rather than wealth or even comfort. Only a few individuals, such as Fidel Castro, Chairman Mao and Joseph Stalin, were able to achieve prosperity by using the rebel leader strategy. However, even these successful rebel leaders endured much deprivation and suffering before reaching high places of power. Humankind is notorious for refusing to pay rebel leaders for conducting revolutions, even though without such revolutions no progress can be made. If being a rebel leader is your main life coping skill, you do not necessarily have to give it up. However, you will probably have to find your *Midas Touch* elsewhere.

The Sick Child

For some children, the best strategy to get love and attention, as well as to avoid responsibilities, is to get sick. Many applied this strategy often in their childhood, some still use it occasionally in their adult life. A small minority are forced by their family dynamics to go as far as making sickness, ineptitude or disability their only successful strategy to get their basic needs met. If this is your case, you may unconsciously resist financial success, which is associated with independence, and in your mind independence and self-sufficiency may be equal to lack of attention and emotional deprivation.

Mr. or Ms. Mediocre

Parents with low self-esteem may feel insecure and inadequate if their children exhibit superior talents and abilities. As a result, such children may get rejected or even punished. Siblings and peers also prefer the mediocre, who will not compete with them for their parents' or teacher's attention and will not threaten their status in their peer group. As a result, some children develop a life strategy of avoiding any success or distinction. As adults, they still associate financial success with rejection, punishment and loneliness.

The life strategy of being mediocre is also frequently developed to avoid responsibilities. When children are smart, responsible and physically able, they are frequently burdened with greater responsibilities by their parents and teachers than their siblings and peers who appear mediocre or exhibit inferior abilities. To escape responsibilities, some children, even exceptionally gifted, may cultivate mediocrity. As adults, they may associate financial success with burdens and responsibilities, and therefore avoid it altogether.

Roles in Peer Groups

Family roles significantly influence the roles that a child may play in his or her peer group, but they do not determine them. Frequently, a child may play one role in his or her family, and a totally different or even the opposite role in his or her peer group. For example, a child who plays the family role of clown may play the role of rebel leader at school. Like your family roles, your peer group roles may also have significantly influenced the formation of life-coping skills that you are using in your adult life.

The Childhood Roles Worksheet

Write down in the blanks the childhood roles that you played in your family of origin and in your peer group. Yours may be one of the common roles described above, or it can be very particular to you and not mentioned here. You may have played more than one role in your childhood. List all of them here.

_____

_____

_____

_____

_____

_____

_____

_____

_____

_____

The Adult Strategies Worksheet

Some of your adult strategies may have originated from your childhood roles from the above list. Write them down in the blanks below.

_____
_____
_____
_____
_____
_____
_____
_____
_____
_____

The Dysfunctional Strategies Worksheet

A life strategy is dysfunctional if it does not bring you the results that you desire, or if it brings such results with mountains of negative side effects. For example, playing the role of clown in your childhood may have provided you with attention and love. Perhaps making your parents and teachers laugh also enabled you to avoid punishment and get the admiration of your peers. In adult life, the role of a clown may still provide you with attention. If done skillfully, such a clown may diffuse many tough situations. However, if you play this role too excessively, no one will take you seriously, and your employment or business will suffer as the result.

So, fill the blanks below with those life strategies from the above list that you consider dysfunctional.

_____
_____
_____
_____
_____
_____
_____

_____

_____

_____

_____

What if all you have are the dysfunctional strategies discussed above? In most cases, this will not prevent you from finding the road of least resistance to prosperity. The beauty of a *Midas Touch* is that it does not demand psychological or any other kind of perfection, and your weaknesses may be as useful as your strengths in generating a substantial income with minimal effort. In some instances however, achieving your financial goals may involve overcoming or compensating for some of those dysfunctional strategies that significantly interfere with your ability to generate income or lead you to financial failure. Therefore, identify such strategies from the above list, and write down below how they may be preventing you from achieving financial success.

_____

_____

_____

_____

_____

_____

_____

_____

_____

Obviously, the above strategies cannot become your *Midas Touch*. So, reduce "acting out" your dysfunctions as much as you can, while applying other life strategies that can bring you financial success.

In some instances however, such dysfunctional financial strategies may be so deeply ingrained into your psyche that you won't be able to stop "acting them out," no matter how hard you try. In these case, financial psychotherapy may help. (See Chapter Fifteen.)

A Common Family Myth

"Your brother (or sister) is more talented than you are." Many of us have received this or similar programming from our parents in childhood, and we may still believe in it today. However, such statements are rarely true.

Since you and your siblings receive similar genes and a similar upbringing, chances are that your talents, abilities and life strategies will be similar to theirs, and all children in your family may have the same or similar *Midas Touch*. Your siblings may have been encouraged by your parents to develop successful financial life strategies. Naturally, when they grew up they became financially successful adults. You may have not been able to do the same because you were not encouraged to develop these strategies in childhood by your family or your peers. By virtue of your birth order and family role, you were forced to develop other life strategies and other abilities, perhaps not as useful in adulthood as those developed by your siblings. Therefore, the belief in your siblings' superiority is a myth. In a great many, though not in all instances, you might be able to reproduce your siblings' financial success by applying the same strategies as they did.

Siblings' Successful Financial Strategies

In the following blank spaces, write down a list of your siblings' successful financial strategies. Make sure that you do not overlook the instances of their success in investment, gambling, real estate, etc. Check also if they were able to use their social connections for business or professional advancement.

_____

_____

_____

_____

_____

_____

_____

_____

_____

Siblings' Faulty Financial Strategies

In the blank spaces below, write down a list of your siblings' faulty financial strategies that could include occupations or businesses in which they worked hard for low wages, as well as a list of their losses due to poor investment, theft, lawsuits, sibling rivalry, wars, revolutions, civil unrest, economic volatility, natural disasters, failed businesses or anything else.

_____

_____

_____

_____

_____

_____

_____

_____

_____

★ ★ ★

Perhaps you have already developed a few interesting ideas about your *Midas Touch* by observing your family's financial successes and failures in Chapters Six through Eight. If so, the following chapters will help you clarify these ideas.

What if you still do not have a clue? Then, you belong in the large camp of those who cannot find their *Midas Touch* in their families. While it is common to receive a *Midas Touch* via the *family transmission process*, in many instances, this does not happen. The unfortunate truth is that due to the harsh socio-economic conditions that many families had to endure, you may not be able to find a single financial strategy from your family repertoire that would be even remotely close to a *Midas Touch*. In this case, you could not discover your *Midas Touch* by observing your family patterns for a simple reason—it has never been there. If this is your case, do not despair. Besides observing the patterns of your family of origin, there are many other ways to discover your *Midas Touch*, which will be discussed in the following chapters.

CHAPTER NINE

Family and Profit

This chapter may invoke indignation in many of my readers who may interpret its content as blatant instructions on how to deceive and manipulate one's family for personal gains. This interpretation is not correct. The financial strategies presented below are *not* based on developing a dependency relationship between family members, but instead on mutual interdependency between them. Such strategies are not based on manipulation, but on a fair exchange.

I am aware, nevertheless, that this chapter's material may bring up your dependency issue. So let's deal with them from the start.

Dependency Issues

With the exception of Native Americans, Eskimos and Hawaiians, the United States' inhabitants are either descendants from immigrants who cut their ties with their native mother countries or are recent immigrants themselves. This perhaps explains why we as a nation value independence and self-sufficiency as our greatest virtue, and some of us move from our parents' home and become financially independent in our late teens. Even our Revolutionary War, fought for independence from Father King and Mother England, can be interpreted as a mass adolescent rebellion. (I am happy that this rebellion succeeded, and the great nation of the United States of America emerged as the result!)

It is common in our country that children move from coast

to coast to get away from their parents, and come back twice a year on Thanksgiving and Christmas. However, a thousand miles' separation cannot free you from your parents' influence, and you may still be using various financial strategies developed in early childhood that are based on your relationship with your parents. If one of these strategies is your *Midas Touch,* then trying to apply it may bring up dependency issues.

These dependency issues are sticky. They hold on to us wherever we go. It appears that God, Goddess, evolution or some other forces, natural or supernatural, created us in such a way that we are usually compelled by our own subconscious to act out our dependency issues again and again, until they are resolved. So, if you still have unresolved dependency issues with your family of origin, which is quite common, you are likely to attract managers similar to your parents and co-workers or customers similar to your siblings. As a result, you may be forced to confront your dependency issues at your job site or in your business. Unfortunately, your managers, co-workers or customers will not care about your issues and therefore won't be helpful in resolving them. This makes the resolving of your dependency issues at your job or in your business not only difficult, but also pretty dangerous to your employment or business success.

Therefore, in some instances dealing with your issues at their source, which is your family of origin, may be much easier than at your job or in your business.

If you decide to depend on your family for your financial or professional success, you will be in good company. Quite a few of the most competent Roman emperors, such as Augustus, Claudius, Hadrian and Marcus Aurelius, achieved their fame, glory and wealth through their family. Likewise many prominent Americans, including Franklin D. Roosevelt and John F. Kennedy, used their family connections to make it to the top.

Hopefully, I have convinced you by now that there is nothing wrong in using your family for profit, especially if are able to provide something in exchange.

Still unconvinced? Then, the strategy discussed in this chapter probably is <u>not</u> your *Midas Touch*. You may still discover many good ideas about your *Midas Touch* in the following chapters. Read through this one, nevertheless, just to discover what you may be missing.

And here are some of the strategies for using familial relationships for profit.

Let Your Parents Pay for It

Your parents may be willing to pay for your student loan, or your first house down payment, or your health insurance. They may also help you financially in starting your own business, or in sending your kids to better schools. There are always strings attached, and you will usually have to do something in return. As in every business transaction, you need to evaluate the *cost/benefit ratio*, and either enlist your parents' help or decline it. (*Cost/benefit ratio* here refers to the emotional and psychological cost involved, weighed against the financial and non-financial benefits to be gained.)

Did your parents receive any financial assistance from their parents? If yes, what kind, under what conditions, and what were the strings attached? You may expect that this pattern will be repeated with you. Also, check if this strategy can be applied to your partner's parents.

The Family Business

If you ever worked in your family business, what was your reward/effort ratio? Include in this ratio the possibility of inheriting it all one day. Was there a pattern in your family of children succeeding financially by working in the family business? Was there such a pattern in your partner's family? What about working in your partner's family business, or your partner working in yours? If you find the *cost/benefit ratio* low enough, perhaps your *Midas Touch* can be found in the family business.

Family Connections

Have you ever been able to utilize your family connections for your professional advancement or business development? Is there such a pattern in your family? Can you use your partner's family connections? Or maybe your partner can use yours? What do you have to do in return to express your gratitude? If you find the *cost/benefit ratio* low enough, perhaps your *Midas Touch* can be found in using your family connections for profit.

Inheritance

Is there a significant possibility that you may inherit? Did your parents inherit anything of real value from their parents? What about your grandparents? Were there cases of sizable inheritance in your partner's family of origin?

Like in any business transaction, there are often strings attached in inheriting money, valuable property or real estate, and as in every business, you may have to compete, this time with your relatives or your partner's. As in every business transaction, you need to evaluate the *cost/benefit ratio*. If this strategy is your only *Midas Touch*, the issues that you may have to deal with to apply it may be easier to resolve than the issues that you would have to face daily at your full-time job.

Family Reputation

Case study: Louis Napoleon

One of the reasons Louis Napoleon managed to become France's President and then the Emperor was the name that he inherited from his illustrious uncle. In spite of his obvious talents and abilities, Louis Napoleon was just one of the great many politicians aspiring for the French Republic presidency. His last name distinguished him from this multitude.

* * *

You do not have to come from a royal family or from the presidential families of Bushes, Kennedys, Roosevelts or Adamses to apply this strategy. If your family has a good reputation in certain circles, you may have a competitive edge in getting a job from or striking advantageous business deals with people who either know your parents or have heard about them. The likelihood that this strategy may be your *Midas Touch* increases if it worked for you before even once. Sometimes, it is enough to apply such a *Midas Touch* only once or twice to ensure your financial success for a lifetime.

Finding a Rich Partner

The *Midas Touch* of marrying or cohabiting with a rich partner is not uncommon in both genders. If your previous partners brought you financial success, or you have declined a few marriage proposals from wealthy suitors in the past, this strategy may work for you. This is especially true if there is a pattern of one partner financially supporting another in your family.

In finding a rich partner financial strategy, abuse and manipulation are possible. However, abuse and manipulation can also be found in any human endeavor. There is probably the same percentage of "gold diggers" among partners of the wealthy as among psychotherapists, doctors, car mechanics, waiters or representatives of any other profession. *No human activity is good or evil by itself. Each has a potential for both being highly moral or highly immoral, or anything in between, depending on your execution of it.*

Naturally, this particular *Midas Touch* would have many strings attached to it, perhaps too many. However, you may find as many strings attached in your relationships with poor partners, and even more in your relationships with your bosses, managers, co-workers or clients and customers. Your choice here depends on your perspective and personal preference.

"How do I find a rich and generous partner?" you may ask. There are a few good books written about it. You do not need to read any of them, even though it might be useful. Instead, analyze how you were able to find such partners in the past. If you have observed such a pattern of marrying wealthy partners in your family, what strategies did the "poor" partners apply to find their wealthy counterparts?

Making Him or Her Rich

Case study: Josephine

When Josephine was involved with Napoleon Boenoparte, he was a "nobody" with great potential, which she was able to recognize. We will never know for sure, but most probably Napoleon would never have become the Emperor without her.

You do not have to marry another Napoleon to apply this strategy. All you need is a partner with a good financial potential and your innate ability to help him or her to achieve financial success. For such a partner, you can provide business ideas, emotional support, secretarial and/or cleaning services or conduct a public relation campaign. Or you can become a sounding board, a counselor and a confessor of a sort.

Needless to say that you can only succeed in it if helping your partners to become rich is your *Midas Touch*. Otherwise, your assistance to your partner may still be useful, but will not bring spectacular results to you.

Profiting through Family Worksheet

In the blank spaces below, write down a list of strategies in which you may be able to use your relationships with your family or your partner for professional advancement, business development or profit. Do not hesitate to include the strategies that you successfully applied in the past, which are not discussed above.

_____

_____

_____

_____

_____

_____

_____

_____

_____

_____

Let's Pretend

Most people who work hard to make a buck (or millions of bucks for that matter) get progressively irritated by observing their partners staying home. If you are one of those stay-at-home partners, it rarely matters whether you take care of the house and the children sixteen hours a day, or spend your days on the couch watching TV. Your partner, otherwise loving and supportive, cannot stand the thought that you may be enjoying life while he or she struggles to put bread on the table. This resentment may appear ridiculous to you, especially if you are the one who stays home. Nevertheless, it can lead to marital problems. The income level is irrelevant here, and this issue may arise in poor families as often as in rich ones.

There are two basic strategies to deal with this issue. One applies to cases when the family indeed is in dire need for money.

Then, you will need to get a job or start a business, or utilize some other means to increase income, hopefully using your *Midas Touch* in the process.

The other solution applies to the cases when money is irrelevant (well, mostly irrelevant). Here, the problem is not financial, but psychological. It exists only in the mind of your partner, and your main task is to diminish his or her irritation at being treated unfairly.

An effective strategy for the second solution is a "Let's Pretend" game that requires some acting on your part and a bit of imagination on the part of your partner. While applying this strategy, you will not have to work hard. You probably will not have to work at all. Instead, you only pretend that you intend to do so sometime in the near future. In many instances, this will pacify your spouse or partner. For a while you will hear less of the complaints that he or she works days and nights, while you waste all the money on frivolous things. Even if you are not a good actor, and your pretensions are pretty obvious, your partner or spouse may be unconsciously compelled to participate in this game and kind of pretend that he or she believes you. Yes, ridiculous as it may sound, the "Let's Pretend" game works in a great many instances. The reason is that your partner does not want to feel anxious and irritated. In truth, your partner usually suspects that his or her accusations are unreasonable, and therefore your partner's own unconscious may propel him or her to go for an imaginary solution to an imaginary problem. So, when you pretend that you are working and making money, or at least attempting to do so, your partner will pretend to believe you. You still need to make it convincing enough for your partner to participate in this game.

"Let's Pretend" games may include, but are not limited to, getting counseling with a focus on career change, going to school, joining a professional association, conducting house repairs, starting a home-based business and keeping it at the starting stage forever, or joining a support group with a focus on career or business development.

"Let's Pretend" games may provide long-lasting yet still temporary solutions to your marital problems. For permanent solutions, you have to include a few elements of reality in it, like getting a part-time job for a few hours a week (consulting would be ideal) or indeed starting a home-based business.

As a last resort, you may help out your partner in his or her business. In this case however, you may actually have to work pretty hard, unless you want to risk your primary relationship.

Many may find "Let's Pretend" games immoral, and so do I. Nevertheless, some of us have no problem in playing such games at our 9-to-5 jobs. Therefore, if you are able to pretend to work instead of working at your job site, you may find it a lot more beneficial and less morally degrading to play the same game at home. And, if this will make you feel guilty, you can find real work for a few hours a week.

Part III

THE MIDAS TOUCH OUTSIDE THE FAMILY

CHAPTER TEN

The Uncommon Midas Touch

This chapter's material is based on the premise that nothing in life is accidental. We have already discussed in the previous chapters that one's life follows certain patterns. These patterns, which frequently defy statistical probability, can be explained by heredity, upbringing, cultural conditioning, *Karma, Dharma* or the will of God. Regardless of the explanation, the observation of such patterns in the lives of my students and associates, as well as in my own life, have brought me to the following conclusion: whatever worked for you financially in the past may produce similar financial results repeatedly in the future.

Here I will discuss some of the various successful financial strategies that do not seriously challenge our conventional beliefs. Yet, they are rarely implemented by people around you. That's why I call them uncommon.

If you or anyone in your family ever tried any of the strategies presented below with promising results, one of these successful strategies may become your *Midas Touch*.

Relocation

If you own real estate in the U.S. and are willing to sell it and move abroad, you can become quite wealthy in a great many places around the world. Not only in the jungles of Colombia or in the Himalayas, but also in many quite civilized locations, where the dollar is still king.

At the time of this writing, the median price of a family home fluctuates between $300,000 and $600,000 in the metropolitan areas of New York, Los Angeles, San Francisco and San Diego, depending on the location. Those who own real estate there should know that a decent one bedroom condominium in Paris, close to most architectural and cultural treasures of this magnificent city and a half-day train ride to many European capitals, runs about $130,000. So, if you own expensive real estate in the States, you can easily retire in Paris.

You do not like big cities? Then consider a one-bedroom condominium in Toulouse, a wonderful city in the south of France, for about $80,000.

You do not approve France's foreign policy? What about a three-bedroom house in the most fashionable resort in Argentina, three blocks from the beach, for $30,000.

You do not speak French or Spanish? What about a condo in Florida for $40,000? Not in Miami, and not on the beach, but still in a pretty good neighborhood. Is it too hot for you in summer? Then, there are zillions of cities, towns and villages in the U.S. and around the world that may provide you with everything you want in real estate, culture, nature, entertainment, education and almost everything else for a lot less than you are paying now. The truth of the matter is that if you own a house in the U.S., you can probably exchange it for at least three equivalent houses in many places in Europe, or for a city block in many areas of Africa or Asia. For this money, you can probably even buy a small village or an island in many quite attractive places.

If you sell your home in some areas of the U.S. and move abroad, you will instantaneously become independently wealthy in many countries. Thousands of Americans have done so. You can find small American colonies in Mexico, Costa Rica, Jamaica, France, Spain, Greece, Italy, Thailand and other places that I have never heard of, but you will hopefully find out about.

You do not want to live outside the U.S.? There are still thousands of places in our country where you can live comfortably and yet very cheaply, at least compared with California and other expensive areas like Manhattan, New York. For your information, 2.2 millions of California left the sunshine state in 1995-2000, many of them to seek cheaper real estate in other states.

For many however, a relocation may not be easy. It takes time, effort, money and psychological adjustment. Besides, you may have to learn a foreign language and accept new cultural values. Even with American citizenship there might be local restrictions on where you can relocate or how long you can stay there. However, it may take you ten, perhaps twenty or even thirty years to retire here. Don't you think that the amount of difficulties that you will have to overcome during these ten, twenty, or thirty years at your present job or business will not be far greater than in relocating or even immigrating? Especially if you are as miserable at your job as I was back in the U.S.S.R. in the 1970s. Relocating to the U.S. was a great challenge for me, as well as for hundreds of thousands of others like me, leaving the Soviet Union for the New World. But it was definitely worth it for the vast majority of us.

The likelihood that relocation is your *Midas Touch* significantly increases, if previous relocations have increased your income or if relocation or immigration brought financial prosperity to your family, especially to your parents.

The financial strategy of increasing one's income or finding cheaper real estate through relocation is one of the most commonly applied in the U.S. throughout its history. This strategy may be at least partially responsible for the fact that we are the richest nation on earth.

Almost all of us are descendants of immigrants who were deprived, persecuted or poor in their countries of origin. Most of these immigrants significantly improved their financial situation by coming here. The immigrants' life strategy of seeking life improvement through relocation was applied by the 19th century pioneers who settled the American West. And now, a great number of Americans still move frequently from coast to coast for better jobs, education or housing. Relocation as a financial remedy has worked for millions of Americans since the Pilgrims, and has become a particular quality of our national character. Therefore, relocation may also work for you, at least as a partial solution to your own financial problems.

So, if you think that relocation might be your *Midas Touch*, jot a few notes below on how previous relocations affected you and/or your original family financially, and when and where you may want to relocate:

_____

_____

_____

_____

_____

_____

_____

_____

_____

_____

The Accumulation of Valuable Objects

Case study: Nina

Nina, a former student of mine, sent me the following email: "Here's a great story for your files. Over the weekend I had a conversation with someone about book collecting. I went to my book shelf and found that I had a book that I bought at a book signing in 1987 for $20. It is now worth $500. So yes, money is everywhere. I just can't part with that book though."

I asked Nina if she had ever had similar experiences in her life before. She remembered that a few times she bought a $500 items for $50. She tried to sell them, but did not succeed right away. So, she decided to keep them instead.

It appears that the accumulation of objects of value may be Nina's *Midas Touch*. Especially if you consider the fact that her parents were also good at it.

Nina's life passion is writing, and she is employed as a journalist. However, if the accumulation of objects of value is indeed her *Midas Touch*, it would have taken her only a few months to learn all the tricks of this trade. Just compare this with all the years of education she had to go through to become a journalist.

* * *

Perhaps, you never considered the possibility that the strategy discussed here is your *Midas Touch*. Neither did Nina, until she was encouraged to pay attention to it.

So, if you were able to buy valuable objects for low prices in the past, or if you can trace such an ability in your family of origin, this strategy may be your *Midas Touch*. Such an ability is rarely universal. Some people can apply it with paintings, but not with postage stamps, and others may be lucky with old oriental carpets only.

If you believe that the accumulation of valuable objects may be your *Midas Touch*, write down below the kinds of items that you and/or any member of your family were able to buy and resell at a good profit.

_____

_____

_____

_____

_____

_____

Note: The ability to buy low frequently does not go together with the ability to sell high. If this is your case, you may have to cooperate with others with a *Midas Touch* complimentary to yours. Besides, you can also get attached to the items in your possession and have significant difficulties in parting from them. Remember that the *Midas Touch is the path of least resistance.* Accordingly, if you have to undergo a monumental struggle to let go of the items that you have bought, the accumulation of valuable objects may not be your road to prosperity.

The Production of Valuable Objects

The production of valuable objects is similar to their accumulation, discussed above, except that you produce valuable items for free rather than buy them cheaply. This strategy also involves the problem of distribution that can be similarly resolved. Here, you can also get so attached to your own work that it would feel like a tragedy to sell it. In this case, look for your *Midas Touch* elsewhere.

If you and/or any member of your family were able to make valuable objects in the past and then profitably sell them, write down below the kinds of items which you or your family had created and how such items were sold.

_____

_____

_____

_____

_____

_____

_____

_____

_____

_____

Real Estate

In principle, investment in real estate is similar to the accumulation of objects of value discussed previously. It is also similar to investing in stocks, discussed in the next chapter. Sometimes, the *Midas Touch* in buying low, holding for a long time and then selling high will operate in all three areas: accumulation of objects of value, investment in stocks and investment in real estate. Most of us though, can only succeed in one specific field, and those successful with stocks may be mediocre in real estate and vice versa.

So, if you and/or the members of your family of origin have been previously successful in buying real estate low, and then selling it high, write down below the kind of real estate bought (commercial, residential, single family home, condo, foreign, etc.), and the strategies applied to buy and sell it. Chances are that similar strategies will produce similar results. Besides buying and selling houses, check also your own and your family's history in dealing with land, finding good apartments with low rent, property management, or anything else related to real estate.

_____

_____

_____

_____

_____

_____

_____

_____

Reducing Spending

The advantages of reducing spending are obvious, and many of us can cut our expenses at least by a quarter, (many—by half, and some—by hundreds of times) before we have to give up the basic features of our comfortable lifestyle. As a nation, Americans are the greatest consumers of energy and resources and the greatest producers of garbage. Unfortunately, for most people the strategy of spending reduction will not work. Many of us may end up spending more money, while trying to spend less of it. The reason for this is that money has become a metaphor for a great many things such as survival, love and power, to name just a few. Frequently, it is much easier to make more money than to spend less of it. Unless spending reduction is your innate *Midas Touch*, it is not worthwhile to struggle with this powerful web of cultural conditioning associated with our eternal and conspicuous consumption.

However, for a select few, reducing spending may do wonders. This strategy may be your *Midas Touch* if you were able to successfully apply it before, or if frugality was considered a virtue in your family of origin. So, if you believe that being frugal my be your *Midas Touch,* jot down below a few ideas on which of your expenses you can reduce and by how much.

_____
_____
_____
_____
_____
_____
_____
_____
_____
_____

Employment

During your work history, you probably have held dozens of jobs. If you have not, you probably will. Even if you spend all your working life in one company, you will probably still move up the professional ladder with years of experience, therefore changing jobs within the company. Obviously, various jobs amount to different pay, and with the same 40 hour a week schedule, the actual work load would also differ. You may have noticed that at some jobs you got paid quite well, even with little education or experience. Or perhaps, the actual workload was so small, that you were paid to read your books or play on the internet. The following case study will provide an example.

Case study: Zara

Zara worked as a receptionist part-time earning $10 per hour. Her work load was very light, and during her 20-hour work week, she rarely worked more than 10 hours. The remaining 10 hours, Zara spent doing editing and proofreading for her private clients, which had nothing to do with her job, and for which she got paid separately, about $30 per hour. Zara's weekly income included, both the $200 of her salary and $300 from her editing business. This resulted in a total of $500 a week, $25 per hour, plus medical and dental insurance.

* * *

You have probably noticed that your financial success varies from industry to industry. Your salary raises, promotions, bonuses and benefits may have been dependent on the company size. You may have done better when working independently, or as a part of a team. Or perhaps, you make more money when working in close proximity to your bosses or supervisors, so that you can impress them with your dedication. And your "luck" may have depended on zillions of other factors that I have never heard of.

So, list below the jobs, industries and other specifics of your profession, where you made the most money with the least effort, and where your actual pay per hour was relatively high.

_____
_____
_____
_____
_____
_____
_____
_____
_____
_____

Consulting

Consulting may be a logical development of your present career. As a consultant you can get paid a lot more for your expertise than at your present job, and if you have developed good business and/or personal relationships with your potential clients, your job security will be about the same as now when you are employed. If you worked as a consultant before, you already know what financial successes and failures consulting may bring. If you are new to consulting, the list above that reflects your success in employment, may give you a good hint as to where you may succeed as a consultant as well, or if you can succeed in it at all.

Were there successful consultants in your family of origin? If yes, in what industries? How did they manifest success? How did they find clients or advertise their services?

Summarize the results of your research on the following page. List the industries where you may become a successful consultant, as well as any consulting specifics that can bring you prosperity.

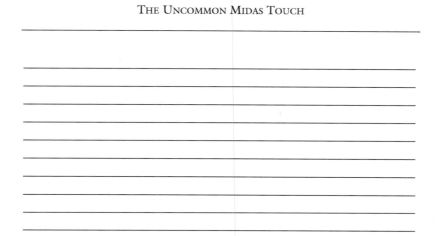

Businesses

In many instances, the skills of generating above average income are transferable from working at jobs to owning businesses. If this is your case, the job worksheet above may give you a few hints on how you can improve your business's financial performance by applying your successful financial strategies as an employee.

If you have been involved in your business for a while, you may have noticed that the business' financial performance may depend on its size, on the type of clientele, and on almost anything else. Frequently, the relationship of the factors is paradoxical, and not what you may reasonably expect. Such a relationship may even defy the law of statistical probability, as illustrated by the following case.

Case study: Allen

Allen's first job in the U.S. was a dishwasher. In a few years, he became the successful owner of a real estate agency, with more than a dozen agents working for him. Allen presumed that since his agents shared with him a portion of their commissions, which amounted to thousands a year of profit from each of them, with more agents he should make more money. Unfortunately, this did not prove to be true. He noticed that

117

with fewer people working for him, his total income would go up. He started letting go of his employees one by one, and eventually found his optimal success formula. Allen's profit was the greatest with only two people working in his office, he and his secretary! With this formula, he lost thousands of dollars coming from his agents' commissions. However, free from the burden of managing and training his staff, he was able to make a lot more himself, while cutting on business expenses.

* * *

Please list below the conditions under which your business produced the highest income with minimal investment or effort. Ask yourself: were you doing better as a solo owner or in partnership? Were you more successful in small, medium or large businesses? In what industries did you do best? What financial strategies worked for your business in the past? List all the elements of your previous successes, even those that may be considered irrelevant by your associates.

_____

_____

_____

_____

_____

_____

_____

_____

_____

_____

Predicting New Trends

You may have wondered whether your professional journey would be affected by the forthcoming technological innovations, changes of fashion, or political and economic upheavals. Nevertheless, I would bet that, like most of us, you make your career choices on the premise that the present state of affairs will probably never change dramatically enough to affect your income. The same is true in business. Most small business owners cannot even imagine that some future trends may ruin their businesses or unexpectedly make them rich. Yet, there are only two sure things in life, death and taxes; the rest is constantly changing. However, there are a few of us who do not just wonder about the future, but also make successful career and business decisions based on their ability to predict future economic and political trends. One of these individuals is discussed below.

Case study: "Country Girl"

"Country Girl" came to the San Francisco Bay Area in the early 1980s. She was a computer nerd, unable to wear high heels or use make-up. Even though she was pretty and intelligent, our "Country Girl" felt quite awkward at social occasions. She could not gossip, flirt or look sexy. That's why her friends, sophisticated urbanites, called her "Country Girl." In spite of her perceived social handicaps, our "Country Girl" had one great asset: her ability to anticipate the future economic and cultural trends, and then act on her hunches, going to the right place at the right time.

Prior to arriving in the San Francisco Bay Area, she had graduated from a computer school with a certificate in computer programming. She was able to figure out with remarkable accuracy that Silicon Valley would be the area where her new profession would be in greatest demand in the coming years. How was she able to do this? She could not tell. Perhaps, she was led there by her intuition. Perhaps, she was just lucky. Whatever it was that inspired her decisions, she arrived in the Bay Area just as the computer boom began to take its shape, and computer programmers were in demand.

On her first job as a programmer, her annual salary was already $25,000, which was the equivalent of about $50,000 in 2004 due to inflation. This was quite an improvement compared with her previous job as a waitress. A year later, our "Country Girl" started a consulting business of her own, and in a few more years, her income became astronomical.

Apparently, her *Midas Touch* was a combination of two skills: her innate talent in computer programming and also her ability to anticipate future economic trends.

* * *

This "Country Girl" was not the only person who had chosen her profession in anticipation of future economic changes. Russian computer programmers, Filipino nurses, Pakistani taxi drivers, and countless others from all corners of the world have deliberately chosen their professions to partake in America's economic boom.

Perhaps, you or the members of your family of origin have been able to foresee what professions or businesses would be in great demand in the near future. In this case, this predictive ability may be your *Midas Touch*. To make it work though, you have to possess at least above average abilities for such occupations or businesses. Otherwise, your chances for great success will be very slim.

If you pay attention to the news, you may be able to discover a few future trends, especially if they are likely to occur in the fields you are already familiar with. Thus, I am pretty sure that financial consultants, gerontologists and all other occupations that deal with the aging baby boomers will be in greater demands for a few decades. In the field of counseling, I can foresee the increasing demand for life purpose counselors, personal coaches, financial psychotherapists and financial astrologers.

You do not have to be psychic to predict that soon our nation will not be able to cope with the ever increasing cost of health care. In a few decades, a great portion of our population won't be able to access the most modern miracle treatments to cure their ills. Many of us will be forced to choose the less expensive alternatives to modern medicine, such as fasting, diet, herbology, ayurveda, hypnosis, and spiritual healing. In traditional medicine, the focus will be on cost efficiency. The practitioners able to provide more affordable treatment will be in demand. So will be specialists in prevention and self-help, as well as those providing inexpensive yet effective medications. If you already work in one of the fields discussed here, your knowledge and skills may be in great demand in a decade or so. In this case, you will have to compete with modern medicine by providing equal or better cures for much lesser cost. Even here, you have to posses a *Midas Touch* in these fields to make it work for you financially.

Future Trends Worksheet

Do you have any knowledge or insight on what professions will be in great demand a few years down the road? If you do, list these professions in the blanks below.

_____

_____

_____

_____

_____

_____

_____

_____

_____

Can you predict what products will be in great demand in the near future? If you believe that you can, what kind of businesses can you start right now to fill this demand? If you already own a business, how can you restructure your business to respond to these future demands? Write down your answers in the blanks on the following page.

_____

_____

_____

_____

_____

_____

_____

_____

_____

_____

eBay

No profession remains in great demand forever. Many computer programmers found this out when they lost their $100,000-a-year jobs. Many of them soon got rehired by the same companies, which were willing to reinstate them in their former positions, but with much lesser salaries.

So, we no longer worship computer programmers. The recent economic trend has produced new ways to generate high income with minimal effort: internet sales. One of the most popular of them is eBay, which is the subject of Adam Ginsburg's book, *The zWay to eBay*. According to Mr. Ginsburg, on eBay, a corvette is sold every three hours, a diamond ring every six minutes, and a digital camera every 60 seconds.

Do we all have to give up our businesses or quit our jobs and start doing business on eBay? Probably not. First, most of us do not have the innate skills in sales, and in internet sales in particular. Second, by the time you get some expertise in the eBay use, it might be too late. Too many people already know about eBay and are rushing to make a fortune there. Unless you have a reason to believe that selling on eBay is your *Midas Touch,* your chances of repeating the grand success of those who got there first are slim. However, if you do not care about great profits and are just interested in a modest income, which you can produce without stepping outside the door, eBay may still be for you.

I suggest that you first read Adam Ginsburg's *The z Way to eBay* or attend his class in San Francisco's Learning Annex. You can probably find similar courses in your area. Also visit eBay's website at www.eBay.com to see how it works.

Besides selling on eBay, there are many other opportunities to sell various items via internet, such as Amazon.com for example. However, you might do better by exploring the new openings to make big money that are just emerging, rather than those known to all.

If you believe that selling via internet is your *Midas Touch,* or if you just want to make money staying at home and playing with your computer, what products can you sell on eBay or through other internet channels? Write down your answers in the blanks below.

_____

_____

_____

_____

_____

_____

_____

_____

_____

_____

Missed Opportunities

Your *Midas Touch* can also be discovered through analyzing the opportunities for generating considerable profit that you have missed. Perhaps you refused a job offer from a start up company that soon became a multinational corporation. If you have accepted the offer, you would be making about $100,000 a year by now, which would have doubled your present salary.

Or perhaps in the 1970s you decided that investing in technology stocks was too risky, and the stocks that you were considering have increased in value sky high in the 1990s. Or you have missed multiple opportunities to invest in real estate, and you are still renting, waiting for the real estate bubble to burst. Opportunities similar to those presented to you in the past are likely to come around again in the future.

To make sure that you will not miss these opportunities again, list such missed opportunities below:

_____
_____
_____
_____
_____
_____
_____
_____
_____
_____
_____

CHAPTER ELEVEN

The "Immoral" Occupations

Here, we will not discuss robbery, theft, prostitution, drug dealing or any other criminal activity. Instead we will talk about investment, stock trading or speculation, and gambling. More than any nation on earth, Americans are open almost to anything that can generate money. Even bank robbers and hired killers become the admired characters of our popular movies. However, there is still a sizable minority who believe that any occupation not involved in producing goods or rendering services is immoral, and such professionals as investors, traders or gamblers are cheats. That is why "immoral" here comes with quotations marks. Such points of view can be found not only among communists, anarchists and religious fundamentalists, but also among investors, traders and gamblers themselves. Some of them, in spite of good profits, consider their occupations immoral and their lives wasted.

Let's examine the matter closer and perhaps move some of the moral dilemmas out of the way.

Moral Dilemmas

Just thinking about gambling as a main source of one's income can make anyone insecure. In addition to insecurities, various moral dilemmas may also arise in relationship to gambling. To a lesser degree, they also arise in relationship to stock market speculations or investments of any kind.

Many Americans like to gamble at least occasionally. Nevertheless, we look at gambling as a vice, perhaps not a very serious one. We also look at professional gamblers as potential criminals, cutthroats of a sort who profit from others' weakness. Nothing is further from the truth. Actually, all three professional gamblers that I counseled were not only law-abiding citizens like you and I, but also exceptionally good-hearted men, honest, reliable and well respected by their friends and associates. And so were other gamblers who they introduced me to. Of course, some professional gamblers do have a criminal record. However, I would bet that gamblers break the law no more often then the representatives of other occupations do.

In my youth, I was indoctrinated by communist propaganda into believing that investors, stock traders and speculators are evil parasites who do nothing productive, yet manage to appropriate the lion's share of the national income, thus stealing from farmers and industrial workers. For years after my immigration to the U.S., I still believed in those lies. I was not alone with such beliefs. Many are still convinced that money should be received in exchange for goods produced or services rendered, and those who do not produce or serve are immoral tricksters and manipulators, who must be punished if not by law, at least by God in the afterlife.

Indeed, money is still a means of exchange for goods and services, but this exchange is no longer fair, as it has not been fair for thousands of years. Even at the time of the Emperor Diocletian, half of the Roman citizens were bureaucrats, employed by the government and far removed from production of goods or rendering useful services. From the communist point of view, all these people were parasites who sucked blood from the nation. Now in the U.S., only 2% of the population are employed in agriculture, feeding the rest of us. Many, if not most of us, are either involved in making each other buy things; or we provide those involved in sales and marketing with material and logistical support. Even in health care, some doctors and many nurses spend a great deal of their time filing out insurance and legal forms, not to mention the army of medical clerical workers who do the same full time.

I am not critical of our American way of life. I love it, and am proud to be an American. Nevertheless, I am not blind to the fact that making money has become our nation's and the world's *educational game*, a kind of virtual reality far removed from the fair exchange of goods and services. In this reality, money inspires each of us to show the best or the worst of what we are made of, and our morality or immorality does not really depend on our occupation.

Yes, you can find immoral gamblers, greedy speculators, or investors concerned only with the bottom line. However, you can also find greedy doctors, manipulative psychotherapists, and according to the popular opinion, plenty of dishonest elected officials.

Yes, if you are involved in gambling, speculating, trading or investing, you may not do anything useful for mankind. However, you also do not produce as much garbage, and do not pollute the environment as much as the average industrial or agricultural worker. You also will not harm as many trees as the average clerical worker, endlessly producing tons of papers. Besides, if you become independently wealthy through such "immoral" occupations, you will be able to donate to good causes, and have time for activities that you consider highly moral.

Does this sounds like justification? Perhaps it is. One can argue, for example, that stock traders may be responsible for the environmental pollution indirectly by investing in industries responsible for producing the world's garbage. One can also argue that we all are collectively responsible for industrial pollution and global deforestation. Similar arguments and justifications can arise in any occupation and in any activity. It appears that gamblers, traders and investors are not morally inferior or superior than those involved in other occupations. They are simply human beings following their chosen professions to make a buck like all of us.

Investment

In principle, investment is similar to the accumulation of valuable objects discussed in the previous chapter. The main difference is that in investing you do not buy objects of value, but you buy their metaphors instead, which are called now stocks, shares or bonds. Another difference is that in investing you become a co-owner of a company and share in its fortune as well as in its misfortune. Frequently, but not always, the *Midas Touch* of buying low, holding for a while and then selling high will operate in both the accumulation of valuable objects and investment.

So, if you were able to make money buying stocks or bonds in the past, or if you invested in your friend's business successfully, or if you can trace a pattern of successful investment in your family of origin, investing may be your *Midas Touch*. Such an ability is rarely universal. Most can succeed with it only within a limited scope. Thus, you may be successful investing in the family business, but may fail with investing in high risk start-ups. Or you may do well investing in mutual funds, but not in foreign government bonds.

If you believe that investing may be your *Midas Touch,* write down below the industries where you or your family were able to invest with profit. Chances are high that similar investments will consistently produce similar results.

_____

_____

_____

_____

_____

_____

_____

_____

_____

_____

Trading Stocks

Trading stocks is similar to investing in stocks, except here you hold these stocks for weeks or months rather than years as in investing. Again, successful long-term investing does not guarantee success in trading stocks and vice versa.

So, if you were a successful stock trader in the past and/or there is a pattern in your family of origin of trading stocks successfully, then this strategy may indeed be your *Midas Touch*.

Write down below the list of stocks that you successfully traded and the industries that they belong to, such as health care, aviation, computers, biotechnology, etc.

_____

_____

_____

_____

_____

_____

_____

_____

Stock Market Speculation and Gambling

Technically, stock market speculations appear similar to stock market trading, but psychologically they are not that similar. With stock market speculations, stocks are held very briefly, and the speculators go after an immediate financial gratification. The successful skills of stock market speculators are similar to those of professional gamblers, and the *Midas Touch* in one of these fields is likely to operate in another.

So, if you or your close relatives have been successful either in stock market speculations or in gambling, write down below the list of stocks in which you or your relatives made money. List also the industries that these stocks belonged to. If you gamble, list the type of gambling (cards, roulette, slot machines, horse races, etc.) in which either you of your family profited from.

_____
_____
_____
_____
_____
_____
_____
_____
_____
_____

Note: In some forms of gambling (the state lottery for example), the odds of winning much are so low that even a *Midas Touch* in gambling may not make any difference.

* * *

"What if I often make a lot of money by trading stocks and as often lose as much?" you may ask. Then, trading stocks may still be your *Midas Touch*. However, you have to significantly modify or eliminate the elements of your trading strategy that cause your financial losses. You may also have to deal with your fear of losses, or learn to let go of your attachment to the shares that you have held for years. Trading risky stocks that rise very fast is like riding a train destined to crash. Such a train can still carry you very far and very fast. If you try to get off the train at the moment of the crash, you are likely to crash with it. So, you have to learn to leave such trains way before they crash. Another option is to trade only stocks of established companies that do not drop in value that rapidly and usually give you ample advance warnings before they crush.

Gambling as an Addiction

Yes, gambling can and frequently does become an addiction. I have provided counseling services to three professional gamblers. One of them is presented in the following case.

Case study: Gus

Gus loved all kinds of gambling for the intellectual stimulation and entertainment that he derived from them. Casinos provided Gus an opportunity for socializing and gave him a sense of community, perhaps even a family of sorts that would accept him unconditionally. Gambling was also a great distraction, a temporary escape from life's pressing problems. As you may guess, Gus was a likely candidate to become addicted to gambling, and he did.

At times, Gus could play very well, on the level of the best professional gamblers. However, winning required discipline, and discipline was no fun. Gambling with discipline would become hard work, with all the thrill of gambling totally lost. Like most gamblers, Gus preferred excitement to discipline. As a result, he began losing substantial amounts, while gambling compulsively, "just for fun." This forced him to seek treatment and he consulted me. In counseling, Gus realized that he was an addict. However, he did not choose to give it up altogether. What he did give up was the impossible dream that gambling would ever become both his main source of income and simultaneously his entertainment. Now, he still occasionally gambles to escape from life pressures, but he works for the government to make a living. He also became successful in trading stocks, which is now a fairly consistent source of his supplementary income.

131

If you, like Gus, are addicted to gambling, with occasional spectacular wins accompanied by consistent losses, then gambling is definitely not your *Midas Touch*. Even if you break even, or make a small profit in it, still this is not your path of least resistance. Addiction and profit rarely, if ever, go together.

* * *

You could not find your *Midas Touch* in the "immoral" occupations? Well, let's go to the next chapter to explore other possibilities.

CHAPTER TWELVE

Social Skills

The financial strategies discussed in this chapter are based on superior communication and social skills. Here, it is not your expertise, but your special skills in relating that make the difference between success and failure.

Many of my readers may feel uneasy while reading this chapter. Naturally, some may interpret its content as instructions on how to deceive and manipulate people for personal gains. It is definitely not so. Please withhold your judgment until the end of the chapter.

Social Connections for Profit

Marketing is a fairly recent strategy of business promotion that became widespread at the end of the 19th century. Now the majority businesses do at least some marketing to attract clients and customers. Some of them spend more on marketing than the actual production. Nevertheless, it is still through personal connections that many business contracts are obtained, especially the most lucrative ones.

The same situation exists in the job market. Even though many of us find employment by mailing resumes and filling in job applications, probably as many obtain jobs, especially good ones, through personal connections.

There are numerous strategies that people apply, often but not always unconsciously, to use their social connections for their career advancement or business development. Here are a few such strategies that I have observed in my students and associates.

The Entertainer

Suppose you are great at drawing attention to yourself at social events. Or you are the star of every party, entertaining other guests with your wits or your looks, or with any other quality of yours that people find amusing. If so, playing the role of the entertainer at social gatherings may be your *Midas Touch*. In this case however, the ability to get attention is not enough, even if you become really popular. You must also have an innate skill to use your popularity in getting ahead financially or professionally. If the "entertainer" strategy is not your *Midas Touch,* your ability to outshine others may be irrelevant, and occasionally even detrimental to your financial success, as illustrated below.

Case study: Julius

After quitting his engineering career, Julius became a sort of celebrity figure. It all began at cocktail parties, where he captured attention with his stories about his new exotic occupation as an astrologer.

Being at the center of attention was new to Julius. He was still shy and far from eloquent in his speech. Nevertheless, like many narcissistic personalities, Julius had an innate talent for story telling. Being a true believer in his own stories, he made an especially strong impression on young and naive women in mild emotional distress. They were allured by his promise that with astrology he could help them to meet their "Prince Charming" or find their "dream" job.

A few people, who met him at the parties, requested an astrological consultation or two, and satisfied, referred their friends to him. Thus, Julius began his career as an astrologer.

A year later, Julius still enjoyed attention at the parties. As his astrological practice grew, Julius became more confident in his abilities and more eloquent in his speech, which allowed him to dominate the conversations at every party that he attended. Julius, previously quite modest, became an arrogant and obnoxious, convinced of his power and uniqueness. His popularity grew, and soon Julius attracted a small circle of followers.

A paradoxical phenomenon took place, however. The increased popularity, and even a little fame which resulted from his initial success, did not increase Julius' business. On the contrary, the first few months were his best, followed by years of struggling with poverty. Julius got at least a dozen referrals from people that he met at those parties in the first two months of his career, and only two (2!)—in two subsequent years. Perhaps, he scared people away by being too bright, or too knowledgeable, or too self-centered and obnoxious. Being the center of attention fulfilled his emotional needs, but not the financial ones. Apparently, Julius could play the role of "an entertainer," but, for whatever reasons, he could not apply this strategy for profit. Obviously it was not his *Midas Touch*.

The Bartender

Bartenders are known to serve as counselors, confidants or even confessors for their clientele, who often visit bars in times of despair and unload the content of their troubled souls. Many bartenders serve as magnets bringing business to their establishments. Besides bartenders, there are numerous other professions, such as hair dressers, masseurs, grocery store owners, taxi drivers, doctors, dietitians, etc., who can utilize this strategy for profit.

The "bartender strategy" can also be successfully used with friends either at social gatherings, or by phone.

If playing a "bartender" for your friends is your *Midas Touch,* the ability to listen and give advice is not enough, even if you become better than a professional counselor or priest. You must also have an innate skill to get your friends, who use you in getting free counseling, to reciprocate by purchasing your goods and services or promoting your business. If the "bartender" strategy is not your *Midas Touch,* the recipients of your free counseling services may want to reciprocate in kind by counseling you.

Home, Sweet Home

Case study: Joan

Joan's home was open for a party every evening. Her numerous friends and acquaintances, as well as their friends and family members, all were welcome to her house seven evenings a week, including weekends and holidays. No advance notice was required. Free food and alcohol were served abundantly, most of it supplied by the regulars.

Joan became a neighborhood mama, providing a few hours of family atmosphere for those of her neighbors and friends who were disenfranchised, socially isolated or bored. Her numerous guests formed a loose informal association with multiple functions, which included psychological and business consulting, employment and match-making services, word of mouth marketing and internet cafe. All such functions were performed informally in the course of the social interactions that occurred every evening.

Joan was the main beneficiary of her not quite selfless community services. Besides being a household item distributor, she was also the owner of a small catering company. Most of those who attended her parties bought her household products, and some hired her to provide catering for parties and events. Naturally, their relatives and friends also became Joan's clients as well. Needless to say that all her business came from her parties. The parties even provided cheap labor for her catering services since she hired only her regulars as waiters and cooks.

Obviously, the "home, sweet home" strategy is Joan's *Midas Touch*. Yours might be similar to hers, even if you choose to conduct it on a smaller scale. If you love to entertain guests in your home, but cannot use your hospitality for profit, this strategy is obviously not for you. Neither can you use this strategy if the idea of mixing business with social events offends you. You can still enjoy giving your parties though.

Acting on a Tip from a Friend

Case study: Elaine

You have already met Elaine in Chapter Three, and hopefully remember that she loved her profession as a Breema practitioner, but made most of her money as an interpreter. Here is how she became an interpreter. Through a chance encounter, she met an interpreter on the beach. The interpreter was a friend of a friend of a friend, and this meeting on the beach was their first and last meeting face to face. Later on, this interpreter gave Elaine a ten-minute phone consultation about the field of interpreting. Immediately after having this conversation, Elaine, fluent in three languages, opened a phone book and made a few job inquiries from the interpreters' agencies listed there. She had her first interpreting assignment within weeks. Thus, Elaine began her new career following a tip from an acquaintance whom she met through her friends. This was not her first time. Three out of six jobs in the last fifteen years, she had found by using this strategy of acting on a tip from an acquaintance met through her friends. Interestingly, she had found the other three jobs also through her social connections.

The strategy employed by Elaine is very simple. Paraphrasing Julius Caesar, we may say: "She sees, she asks, she acts, she gets a job." If you were able to do the same in the past, then acting on tips that you get through your social circle may be your *Midas Touch*.

137

Jobs and Vodka

Case study: Ilya

In case you do not remember, Ilya is me, the author. When I was a lad of seventeen, still living in the great Ukrainian city of Odessa, I got my first job by following a proven Russian strategy for employment. My father gave a bottle of vodka to the chief of a local factory's personnel department. The chief liked the vodka, and I was hired. A year alter, my parents applied the same strategy to secure my second job. They invited their long-term friend and his wife to a very good gourmet dinner, with a lot of vodka of course. This friend was a department chief of a local ship building company. Due to his effort, I soon began working for that company, which was a considerable professional advancement for me.

I am sure that this strategy would have worked wonders for me in the U.S. too. It is too bad I cannot drink vodka.

* * *

The case study above was not a joke or an author's invention. It reflects a legitimate and widely used strategy of achieving success by appealing to the palates of important people; and this strategy can be easily executed even without vodka. There is nothing morally wrong in inviting VIPs to expensive restaurants, and when they get relaxed and hopefully slightly drunk, asking them for a favor or two. Obviously, this strategy is not for you if reading about it invokes indignation and disgust in you.

The Lion King

Case study: Steve

Steve, a literary agent, published author and seminar leader, is the charismatic president of a public speakers' club. He makes no money as the president, and this prestigious volunteer position takes a lot of his time and energy. However, this post makes him a sort of a "Lion King," providing a platform to sell his books and seminars, and to meet the authors whom he may want to represent.

* * *

Such a "Lion King" strategy may work for psychologists, doctors, masseuses, plumbers, electricians, real estate agents, etc. Needless to say that you can only succeed with this strategy, if it is your *Midas Touch*. If it is not, you will end up with a loosing game of excessive responsibilities and little profit. You may even suffer financial losses paying for the glory. You may still enjoy the attention though.

Kin to the Lion King

In every social circle, there are individuals that can be called the centers of power, "Lion Kings of the Jungle" of a sort. They may be distinguished for holding upper management positions in the government or in major corporations, or they may own successful businesses. In ethnic groups or in rural communities, such a "Lion King" may be a local religious figure, mayor, healer, doctor, or any charismatic individual with or without any particular professional or social accomplishments. These "Lion Kings" can connect you with their inner circle, leading to better jobs and great business deals. According to fairy tales, a "Lion King" would always be a person of nobility, courage and good heart and would appreciate the same in servants and followers. You do not need to do much to get their benevolent attention and become their kin. Just show your loyalty and reliability, and hide your desire to outshine your benefactor, then your own financial success is almost guaranteed, especially if the "Kin to the Lion King" strategy is your *Midas Touch*.

This strategy may be appalling to you, especially if you

have it in you to become a "Lion King" yourself. If so, do not even think about trying it. However, this strategy may still work, if you are an independent sort, not afraid to speak your mind in front of authorities. A "Lion King" may appreciate honesty, as long as you do not claim the throne.

So, if you have a good track record in establishing connections with people in power, and using these connections for profit, or if you can see such a pattern in your family of origin, this strategy may be your *Midas Touch*. Be aware though that some "Lion Kings" only appear noble. They may squeeze you like a lemon without giving anything in return.

Reflecting Sunlight

The moon does not have its own light, but shines by reflecting the sun's radiance. All the planets of the Solar system, and their satellites as well, do the same, and so can you.

The "Reflecting Sunlight" strategy is almost identical to the "Kin to Lion King" strategy discussed above. Here, the role of a "Lion King" may be played by your partner, spouse, parent, friend or relative.

Do not take me wrong. While applying this strategy you do not have to give up your individual self for the more successful significant other. This is just a strategy that will affect the way you make money. With its successful implementation, you will have plenty of freedom to express yourself elsewhere.

By applying this strategy, you may lose in the power struggle with your spouse or partner, since this strategy will reinforce his or her leadership position in the relationship. Your alternative though is to seek your income elsewhere. Then, you will engage in the power struggle with your boss or your supervisor, which you will probably lose.

Specialist

Case study: Allen

In the previous chapter, you have read about Allen, a dishwasher who became a realtor. His success was achieved by the following strategy. Allen, a picture of perfect health and vitality, joined a fitness club. The club membership was outrageous, but the wealthy clients whom he picked up there provided him with real estate commissions thousands of times greater than the membership fee.

* * *

Besides real estate agents, this strategy may work for any profession, and in many instances you can substitute Allen's fitness club for extended family gatherings, community events or informal meetings with friends.

If using this strategy you end up providing your relatives and friends with professional services for free, for substandard fees or for credit, this strategy may be a great community service, but it is surely not your *Midas Touch*.

Barter

Informal barter is one of the most common strategies of using social connections for profit. Thus, friends or family members do reciprocal favors for their kin, which may include job referrals, business contacts and valuable information leading to professional and business development. Even if you are not able to reciprocate in kind, you can still provide domestic help, gourmet dinners, baby sitting, or pick up your benefactors from the airport. Needless to say, this informal barter strategy works only if the other side reciprocates.

If you were successful in applying this strategy in the past, or you observed successful use of informal barter in your family of origin, this strategy may be your *Midas Touch*.

Formal barter is common between businesses and non-profit organizations. There are also a few grassroots groups and rural farming communities that are based on bartering goods and services between their members. In any kind of bartering some people constantly win, and others often lose. If you belong to the latter, you can still barter, but bartering is not your *Midas Touch*.

The Hypnotist

The "Hypnotist" strategy is based on a superior ability to conduct the sales of your product or services via social intercourse at parties, extended family gatherings or phone conversation. Depending on your personality, this strategy can be applied as straightforward direct suggestions to buy your product or service, or as subtle self-promotion, skillfully woven into the conversation.

If you were able to get your family and friends to buy your products and services in the past by using direct suggestions or embedded instructions, or you observed the successful use of this strategy by your parents and/or siblings, this strategy may be your *Midas Touch*.

Social Connections Worksheet

In the blank spaces below, write down a list of strategies in which you may be able to use your social connections for professional advancement, business development or profit. Do not hesitate to include social strategies that have not been mentioned above.

_____

_____

_____

_____

_____

_____

Faked Orgasms

Social and sexual intercourse have at least one thing in common: in both you can pretend. In sexual intercourse, you can pretend having great orgasms. This would be more difficult for males, but it still can be done by both genders. Similarly in social intercourse, you can pretend that you are delighted to see so and so, and are genuinely interested in his or her stories. There are significant limitations on how much and how frequently you can fake your enjoyment of sexual intercourse. The same holds true for your social exchanges.

It is a common knowledge that sexual intercourse is not a purely biological act, but contains many social and even spiritual elements in it. It is not as well known that social intercourse is not only a social phenomenon, but also contains many biological components. Thus, during social intercourse, your posture, the way you walk, the minuscule involuntary movements of your face and intonations of your voice will exhibit your true emotions. I have not even mentioned Freudian slips that may betray your intentions at the most inappropriate moments. Neither did I mention your body scents that always reflect your elation, fear, desire or boredom, no matter how recently you took a shower. Such involuntary body motions and scents are so faint that no one is aware of them. Unconsciously though, everyone around you responds to such almost undetectable motions and scents by either being attracted to you or repelled by you. To put it simply, you might be able to successfully fake your enjoyment of social interactions occasionally, but in order to do it consistently, you must like the people you converse with. Otherwise, you are bound to repel the people that you are trying to attract.

Partially Faked Orgasms

If you truly love, or at least are attracted to, your sexual partner, you can easily exaggerate your enjoyment of a sexual act. Who cares then about the big "O"? The same is true for social intercourse. You have to like people in general, and at least respect the persons whose help you are seeking to exaggerate your enjoyment of their company. Chances are that your initial partially faked interest in your influential acquaintances may grow into a real one, once you get to know them better.

True Orgasms

Here is one of your moral dilemmas solved. True orgasms occur naturally and spontaneously. No faking is required. The same is true for individuals able to use their social connections for profit. They do it easily, naturally and usually unconsciously. Most of them are not even aware of their special gift. On the other hand, if you have been a loner all your life, disgusted by the vanity of social events, then using your social connections for profit is unlikely to become your *Midas Touch*.

Sales

Individuals good at sales may apply any of the strategies discussed above in addition to scores of others presented in various sales instructional manuals. You do not have to read them all, if sales on commission is your *Midas Touch*. Instead, in the blank spaces below, write down a list of products you were able to sell at a good profit and a list of strategies that you applied to sell them. If you have never been able to sell anything at all, skip this worksheet altogether.

_____

_____

_____

_____
_____
_____
_____
_____
_____
_____
_____

More on Moral Dilemmas

The idea of manipulating people, especially relatives and friends, for personal gain will not appeal to many people. I admit that I do not like it either. However, the fact is that "you cannot *not* manipulate others," as stated by Bender and Grinder in their book *Frogs into Princes,* popular in the 1980s.

Perhaps manipulation is too strong a word to express the fact that we constantly influence others. And no matter how much you try to communicate objectively and stick to facts, your body language and scent will still betray your true desires. Those listening to you may not be manipulated by your speech, but they absolutely cannot avoid responding subconsciously to your subconscious communication. This occurs in spite of the fact that none of you are aware that such communication is taking place. Let's not worry about influencing others against their will. The fact is that we cannot *not* communicate with others who are in close proximity to us. Even if we do not say a word, our silence is still a form of communication that will influence them. I believe that since we cannot not influence people, we should at least attempt to influence them in the direction of our common interests.

Keep it in mind that most of human communication is subliminal. Verbal communication is only a small part of it. People can lie with words, but it is impossible to lie with their whole being. Therefore, you need not worry about manipulating people. Even if you possess the innate talent to influence people, you can only influence them in the directions that they desire to be influenced. At the worst, you might be able to occasionally and briefly control a few very gullible individuals. This will not produce much of a profit, which will probably discourage you from doing it ever again.

CHAPTER THIRTEEN

Wandering Nomads

The unconventional solutions discussed in this chapter may help you to achieve financial freedom. However, they may require courage, or desperation, or a spirit of rebellion on your part. These solutions challenge one of our most fundamental cultural myths that prescribes the accumulation of valuable possessions, especially real estate, as the only means to personal security and happiness. The majority of us usually reside in one place for a very long time, perhaps for life, and spend more on mortgage or rent than on anything else. So, if you are able to live without modern conveniences, which most people cannot, you automatically get rid of your major expenses on real estate, thus becoming independently wealthy, or at least gaining independence from your full-time job. And this can be accomplished almost overnight.

A Brief History of Property

The concept that security, wealth and happiness is always associated with individual ownership of material possessions and real estate did not come from God. At the dawn of our civilization, property and real estate were communal. No individual could survive on his or her own. Thus, individual property ownership would be suicide for almost anyone who attempted it.

Between 7,000-3,000 B.C., bands of nomads conquered the original agricultural communes, and divided the land and its inhabitants between themselves. From this point in history, humanity was divided into the privileged land and property owners and serfs who hardly owned anything. Thus, we have learned to associate individual property ownership, especially ownership of real estate, with happiness, individual freedom, security, access to food, education, entertainment and medical care, as well as status in the community.

However, there have always been mavericks who never bought into the concept that individual property ownership equals happiness. Such dissidents living outside the mainstream culture included gypsies, Indian yogis, traveling artists, sailors, wandering dervishes, soldiers of fortune, caravan merchants and many others. So, throughout history up to the present, there has always been a sizable minority born for nomadic life, and you might be one of them.

Difficulties in the Beginning

If you are a nomad at heart, living all your life in one place, while keeping a business or job like everyone else, may be dangerous to your mental health. However, the coping skills that you have developed while living a stationary life may not work if you switch to a nomadic lifestyle. In applying a new financial strategy, conventional or unconventional, there will be a period of adjustment, during which you will have to overcome some practical difficulties and also deal with psychological issues and moral dilemmas. If one of the strategies below is indeed your *Midas Touch,* the period of adjustment will be relatively short, and the temporary difficulties of making a transition will be a lot less than a lifetime of drudgery.

The Traveling Consultant

Case study: Ernie

Ernie was an electrical engineer working as a consultant for various companies throughout the continental U.S. He lived and traveled in his motor home, which he always parked on the property of his current employer, thus reducing his rent to zero. Hooking up his motor home to his employer's power, gas and water lines, which was part of his contract, provided him with free utilities. Earning top dollars and paying no rent, Ernie became independently wealthy, working where, when and how much he wanted.

Ernie is not so unusual. There are thousands of people living in mobile homes for significant periods of time. For some, it is seasonal; for others—a preferred way of life.

You do not need Ernie's graduate degree in engineering to follow his footsteps. Writers, public speakers, salespersons, surveyors, woodcutters, construction workers, fishermen, nurses, doctors, plumbers, forest rangers, etc., can easily do the same. This lifestyle is also becoming popular with retired couples, who are finally ready to explore the world. The beauty of this financial strategy is that you can apply it for a few years, during which you may be able to save most of your earnings, and settle down later on.

"This is a lifestyle for a loner," you may say. Not always so, as illustrated in the following example.

Case study: Damitar

Damitar was a piping designer, working as a consultant for various engineering firms in the U.S., while living and traveling in his bus. His life was similar to Ernie's, with a huge difference. In his bus, Damitar was traveling with his wife and their four children. The family was happy, frequently changing locations, living on the road, and occasionally sleeping under the stars. Curiously, when Damitar settled down in California, he and his wife developed marital problems which did not exist while they lived as Gypsies on the road.

Working Abroad

Case study: Alex

Alex was also an electrical engineer like Ernie, earning top wages as a consultant. Unlike Ernie however, he did not live in a motor home. Alex was a family man, a full time permanent employee of a large corporation. Yet, Alex and his wife not only lived rent and mortgage free, but they also lived in luxurious houses with maid service. During fifteen years of his employment, Alex's employer sent him to Chile, India and Brazil. He worked for a few years in each country with all his expenses paid.

You do not need Alex' top qualifications to work abroad. American specialists are highly respected anywhere in the world. Even if you will not earn as much as Alex, your expenses abroad will be so much less than here. You will experience life in different cultures and save money in the process.

Working Aboard

Case study: Svetlana

Svetlana was a musician working on European cruise ships. For years, she traveled around Europe, all expenses paid plus a small salary. All she had to do for it was to look pretty and play her instrument for twenty minutes each evening.

You may not want to spend your entire life on a cruise ship like Svetlana, but this might be an interesting option for a while.

In addition to cruise ships, you can also find a job at mer-

chant ships, airlines or trains. In these situations, you probably won't earn much. Still, all expenses paid and free travel are
worth considering.

The Traveling Merchant

Case study: Sally

Sally was a professional psychic, antiques collector and an
artist. She made a living by selling her goods and services at
various New Age fairs, while living in her bus, in which she followed these fairs throughout the country. Sally never became
wealthy. Instead, she achieved the ultimate freedom to go wherever and whenever she wanted, doing what she felt like doing
at every given moment. Very few, if any, wealthy people ever
achieve the same degree of freedom, which for her was worth
the minor inconveniences of living in her crowded bus. Sally's
lifestyle is not for everyone, but it is a tantalizing option for
some.

* * *

On our huge planet, there have always been large discrep-
ancies in the price of goods and labor in various locations, and
the opportunities for traveling merchants are as abundant now
as in the times of Marco Polo. Needless to say, this strategy is
only for people with the special gift of rapidly adapting to foreign lands and strange cultures and customs. If your grandparents or parents arrived to this country penniless and made
their fortunes as traveling merchants here, then your chances to
succeed with the same strategy are high.

Almost Free Rent

Case study: Jonathan

Jonathan was a successful entrepreneur, who got fed up with his life, sold his business, donated most of his money to charities, and moved to the big island of Hawaii. There, he lived in a tent, hiked around the island, and meditated for a few hours a day. Jonathan was happy with his new life, except that he often felt isolated and bored. So, he applied his entrepreneurial skills to starting a new business, doing what he loved and getting paid for it. Jonathan became a tour guide, showing tourists the spectacular walking trails and sharing his knowledge of the island's history with them.

Besides living in a tent like Jonathan, you can also live in a trailer, bus or motor home. Even a car with reclining back seats may serve as a home, if you can manage with only a few possessions. You can park very cheaply in national and state parks. In some of them, you can park for free.

Living on a Boat

Living on a boat is somewhat similar to living in a tent, motor home or trailer. Here you may find a few great business opportunities. If your boat is big enough, you can do tours and romantic get-aways or accept charter fishing expeditions. Or you can rent your boat out as a vacation spot to provide you with extra income while you travel. This is a real option for those who love life on the water.

Working at Resorts

Case study: Lulu

Lulu was the manager of Club Mediterranee in Mexico. In addition to managing her staff and giving her daily speeches welcoming the guests, she was also a producer, choreographer, and lead singer and dancer at the club's shows, staged every evening. She was constantly busy seven days a week, with only a few hours' break at night. Yet, she loved her life, which was a party all day long. If she ever got bored in Mexico, she knew there were dozens of other Club Meds around the world that would gladly employ her.

* * *

Besides Club Meds, there are thousands of resorts around the globe that hire waiters, maids, housekeepers, cooks, hosts, entertainers, managers, plumbers, construction workers, carpenters and so on. Very few such places would require Lulu's dedication or her artistic qualifications. With some research, you can easily find those with minimal work requirements, free rent and all expenses paid.

You can easily explore such opportunities while on vacation, where you meet and interview people who do this for a living.

Working for Food and Shelter

This financial strategy consists mostly in exchanging your labor, usually but not always manual and physically demanding, for food and simple accommodations. This strategy can be used as a lifestyle or applied temporarily, during major life transitions or while traveling. In this case you will have to work 15-20 hours a week, the rest of it will be your personal time.

I know of a few organizations that widely practice such work for food and shelter exchanges.

The most well known of these are Israeli agricultural communes, called kibbutzim. Those of my fellow Americans who worked there told me that the workweek was about 30 hours, and it was not very demanding. In exchange, they got excellent food, acceptable accommodations, free tours around the country and free courses in Hebrew. Everyone I talked to, had a lot of fun being there. However, Kibbutzim are only for those who believe in the Zionist movement, or at least are not opposed to it. For information on work exchanges in Israel, consult your local Jewish community center or the nearest synagogue. Israel is not the only country where such a work exchange is possible. Many other opportunities exist. Here are a couple of them that I know of.

Through "Willing Workers on Organic Farms" International (http://www.wwoof.org/), you can find work exchange jobs around the globe. A friend of mine went to New Zealand where she got employed through this organization. There, she was doing agricultural labor three hours daily in exchange for food and spartan accommodation. The rest of the time she was free to explore the country.

There is another such organization, called BACKROADS. It provides hiking and biking vacations around the globe, and is frequently in need of cooks, tour managers and travel guides. Food and air travel are paid by the company, camp accommodations are free, and a small salary is a bonus. If you love hiking, biking, camping and traveling, look for BACKROADS in Berkeley, California or for a similar organization in your area.

Working for Causes

Case study: Mary

Mary was a nun, working as a school teacher for an American nonprofit organization that sent her to various Latin American countries. Mary had no interest in accumulating possessions or buying real estate. Money did not interest her either. All she wanted was to help the poor, practice her faith and see new exotic places. And she lived as her heart desired, rent free and with all her expenses paid. Her accommodations were very simple but quite adequate for her taste.

You do not have to be a nun to apply Mary's strategy. It is fairly easy to acquire a trade that would make you employable by the Peace Corps or by various non government organizations, secular or religious. You could also work for the U.N., or for scientific expeditions. In all those jobs, you probably won't get paid much, but food, accommodation, travel and medical care will be provided. Besides, you will be working for noble causes, which by itself can give you sense of destiny that makes life worth living.

Apartment Management

Case study: Nathan

Nathan is the manager of a three-story apartment building in Oakland, California. His salary is small, but living rent free in the San Francisco Bay Area is worth a lot. Nathan rarely works more than a couple of hours a day. His main responsibility is to just be there, watching over the property and being available for emergencies.

* * *

If you have been able to find good places with low rent in the past, or if there is pattern similar to Nathan's in your family, then this strategy can be your *Midas Touch*. If indeed it is, you may be able to acquire a nice place to live, sometimes large and luxurious, in the best neighborhoods for free. No special skills are required, just a reputation of being honest and reliable. The ability to do minor house repairs will be a plus here.

Personal Services to the Rich and Famous

If you are not an alpha male or alpha female, and if you do not mind service occupations, such as cook, personal assistant, governess, butler, driver, nurse, housekeeper, etc., the strategy of providing personal services to the rich and famous may work for you. (In case you do not know, an alpha person is an individual with leadership ambitions and lust for power.) Your salary may not be high, but you will be surrounded by luxury, and food and accommodations will be free. Such positions frequently require very hard work, and instances of blatant exploitation are common. However, if you have manners, immaculate appearance, a good reputation and special skills useful for the rich and famous, you might be able to live in their luxurious homes in exchange for your daily labor. In this case, high self-esteem and the ability to stand up to arrogant people spoiled by fame is a must.

Nomadic Strategies Worksheet

The advantage of all the strategies described above is that you can apply each of them for a certain period, from a few weeks to a few years. Some nomadic strategies are often interchangeable. Thus, if your *Midas Touch* is living on a boat, it might also work in managing apartments or providing personal services to the rich.

So, in the blank spaces below, write down a list of nomadic strategies in which you may be able to use your *Midas Touch*. Do not hesitate to stretch your imagination and include the nomadic strategies not discussed in this chapter.

_____

_____

_____

_____

_____

_____

_____

_____

_____

_____

CHAPTER FOURTEEN

Unconventional Prosperity Tools

This chapter will discuss various business and life coping strategies that can be called *unconventional prosperity tools*. They are unconventional because very few people would ever consider applying them for income increase. Nevertheless, they have been known for centuries as the means to get out of tough financial situations. None of these *prosperity tools* can produce financial rewards by themselves. They can only enhance the effectiveness of your *Midas Touch* or remove obstacles to its use.

Restructuring

This financial strategy is quite common with businesses, big and small, as the last resort to stay afloat, for example after declaring bankruptcy. However, you do not have to wait for a financial disaster to apply at least some restructuring in your own business or profession.

If your business is not as profitable as you would like, make as many modifications in it as you possible can. This may include firing some of your employees and hiring new ones, or moving your business to a new location. You can also identify the dysfunctional parts of your business and change them completely.

If you are dissatisfied with your salary, or if you have not been promoted for awhile, you can either change jobs within the company, or find a different employer, preferably in a different industry or in a different location, or both.

Needless to say, restructuring cannot be applied too often, and not always will it produce a change in your financial situation. If you applied this strategy too frequently in the past, often changing jobs, or if your business is constantly restructuring, and none of it produces substantial financial gains, then another restructuring is unlikely to produce the desired result.

Getting Rid of Clutter

Some people report significant positive changes, including improvement of their financial situation, by simply getting rid of clutter. Just cleaning your desk of old and useless papers may produce a psychological shift in you, leading to a financial breakthrough. Similar results may be achieved by getting rid of old furniture stored in your garage or by thorough cleaning of your office or home. In addition, you can also take your old clothes to the Salvation Army or give away the things you do not use to your friends or neighbors.

You can also encourage your employees to apply this strategy since it may lead to a positive shift in their performance.

Creating a Social Vacuum

The idea behind this strategy is that your present social circle of family and friends is likely to be helping you to maintain your present situation. However, supportive as it may be, your social circle is also likely to resist any of your attempts to improve your life. So, in order to generate a positive change, you may have to significantly reduce—in extreme cases even totally eliminate—your ties to your present social environment. This will place you in a social vacuum that will draw into your life new friends and associates who will be more helpful in achieving your financial goals.

Cutting the Ties that Bind You

As a Marriage and Family Therapist, I help my clients to improve their relationships with their parents, spouses, children, business partners, friends and co-workers. However, I have to admit that some relationships cannot be improved. They will always bring up the issues that cannot be resolved, forever draining the life force from those involved in them. The only solution here is terminating such relationships. Many of my students and clients experienced a tremendous relief when they divorced an abusive spouse, fired a troublemaker, or stopped serving an overly demanding customer. Others regained a sense of well-being after quitting a job with an oppressive boss or quarrelsome co-workers.

Note. Terminating relationships, especially between family members, should not be considered lightly, and applied only when all other means to improve such relationships have been exhausted.

Getting Rid of Ballast

The strategy is also known as the "80/20" strategy. The "80/20" here means that in most money producing activities 20% of your efforts will produce 80% of the results. The remaining 80% of your efforts will be quite inefficient, producing only 20% of the results. Naturally, you will be better off by investing your time and money on the 20% that produce most of the results.

This strategy is frequently applied by airlines, which eliminate less profitable flights when they experience financial difficulties. Major publishing houses also apply a similar strategy. They publish thousands of titles and let them sit on the shelf for a while. A few titles that sell well from the start get promoted and may become bestsellers. The rest of the books that do not sell right away get removed from the stores. In spite of their future sales potential and cultural value, many of them are shredded.

To apply the "80/20" strategy in your business, focus only on the products and services that have produced financial results, and do not spend your time and resources on the rest.

This strategy is frequently applied by stock traders. They buy a number of stocks, observe their performance for a short while, and then sell all those that do not perform, making a profit on the rest.

Cleaning Your Psyche

Besides cleansing yourself of psychological baggage, which will be discussed in Chapter Fifteen, you may find it useful to also clear your psyche from grudges that you may still hold against others. This can be accomplished by affirmations and visualizations, discussed in Chapter Nineteen, or prayers, discussed in Chapter Twenty. Psychotherapy may also help. Forgiving, forgetting and letting go of your grudges will liberate you from your past and assist you in creating a more fulfilling and prosperous life.

Intuition

Many successful people are known to make serious business decisions by following their intuition. They would admit making these decisions following a strong "gut feeling" that would "advise" them on the course of action. It seems that intuition is at least partially responsible for their success.

If you have a proven record of using your intuition for profit, then it may become a great aid to your *Midas Touch*. Be aware though that intuition, like all other qualities, may be field specific. For example, your success in using your intuition in finding parking does not necessarily mean that you can also use it in increasing your income.

Feng Shui

Feng Shui is an ancient science and art of geomancy and placement, developed in medieval China. The principles of Feng Shui can be applied to interior design. According to this system every wall of your house is decorated with specific images of specific colors. You also have to choose home and office furniture of appropriate shapes and colors, and place it in the appropriate location. By rearranging certain areas of your house according to Feng Shui, you can increase your income. Feng Shui also prescribes the use of mirrors, crystals, flowers and in-house miniature waterfalls to improve your chances for financial success.

For some, Feng Shui may produce good results fairly fast, as illustrated in the following case.

Case study: Elaine

Elaine got a book on Feng Shui from a friend, and rearranged her office according to the book's instructions. In the following weeks, her professional status changed from a self-employed solo interpreter to the owner of an interpreting agency. She was also offered a part-time position with health insurance benefits, which she accepted. Soon, her income doubled. Encouraged by her success, her husband also attempted to use Feng Shui to increase his income. With the husband, the results were not nearly as dramatic. There was some modest improvement, but not nearly as spectacular as with Elaine. Apparently, like all other life strategies, Feng Shui does wonders for some people, but not for others.

You can find books on Feng Shui in your local public library or in most bookstores. I personally prefer Master Lam Kam Ghuen's *Feng Shui Manual*.

Changing Your Name

I came to realize the significance of names in the lives of their bearers by watching *Star Wars*. The main character of the saga was Luke Skywalker, which is literally Sky Walker. The meaning of Luke's last name points to his destiny as a fighter pilot and space explorer.

Later on I found out that every name has a meaning. Even if you have no idea what your name means, any time people call you by your name, its sound produces a certain psychological effect on your psyche, which can become quite significant over the years. So, by changing or modifying your name, you may change your life. If you do not like your life, you may alter it by either using your middle name, or choosing a name that reflects a quality that you want to manifest. Curiously, on every spiritual path, a neophyte is always given a new name by his or her master to indicate a transition from one life to another. You can claim to be your own master and do the same.

As an experiment, ask your friends and associates to call you by a different name of your choosing for a couple of months. In addition, you can alter your signature accordingly. Then evaluate if your new name has produced any effect in your life.

Antidepressants

If you are frequently depressed, elevating your mood may also enhance your ability to generate greater income. Regardless of the causes of your depression, anything that consistently lifts your mood, including but not limited to antidepressant medications, may help you to get on your road to prosperity.

By the way, medications are not necessarily the best way to elevate depression. For instance, prozac was considered a miracle performance drug in the 1990s. In reality, medications such as prozac are only about 33% effective, their effect ranging from moderate to remarkable. In comparison, placebos produce the same effect in 25% of the cases. There are numerous other methodologies that may alleviate depression, such as aerobics, walking, dancing, psychotherapy, relocation, dietary changes, etc.

De-Crystallization

This strategy is especially useful when you feel stuck, and all your monumental efforts produce only meager results. To achieve de-crystallization, you have to detach yourself temporarily from your familiar environment and, hopefully, from the familiar way of perception. Relocation, traveling, pilgrimage, vacations and retreats are most appropriate to achieve this purpose. Quitting or changing jobs will also help you to de-crystallize.

In many instances, a weekend retreat to a quiet inspiring location will be enough. Stay solitary or surround yourself with a company of the like-minded. Review this book. Meditate. Pray for a vision. Record your dreams. Engage in sports, or do nothing. The most important point is that you get involved in activities that you normally do not get involved in at your business or home.

If you cannot get away even for a few days, take several half-day vacations from your routine and explore a neighboring city, or a spend a few hours in a movie theater, or visit a friend whom you have not seen for ages, or take a class on a subject that you previously did not have much interest in. What you choose to do does not really matter as long your new activity increases your horizon and helps you to think "outside the box."

Soon, you will be more open-minded, full of new ideas and ready to implement them into practice. If your previous de-crystallizations produced financial improvements, then periodic de-crystallization may become your main *prosperity tool.*

Tithing

This *prosperity tool* came from the field of religion. At the dawn of civilization, our ancestors developed the practice of sacrificing a certain portion of their produce or livestock to the gods, hoping that these gods would reciprocate. This practice evolved through the religions of antiquity and was inherited by the modern ones.

Members of many Christian, Jewish and Moslem congregations, and devotees of various New Age religions as well, usually donate a portion of their income to their temples, churches, synagogues and mosques. Donating 10% of your income to your religious organization seems to be the norm. I have heard and read about numerous claims that such generous donations have multiplied the donors' wealth. Even though such statements cannot be verified, I have enough anecdotal evidence to believe that such practices do work for some people. (See Catherine Ponder's *The Dynamic Laws of Prosperity* for case studies.)

Even if you are not especially religious, giving generously and consistently a portion of your income to others may give a tremendous boost to your self-esteem, triggering your subconscious to propel you towards financial improvement. Besides, being a donor places you in a position of power and respect, which may result in more business or job offers.

To figure out if this strategy can aid your *Midas Touch,* start donating a portion of your income to a religious or a nonprofit organization of your choice periodically. Even if you are really poor and cannot part with any of your money, you can still volunteer your time. Practice this for a few months. If you notice a marked income increase, then you have found your *prosperity tool.*

Prosperity Tools Worksheet

In the blank spaces below, write down a list of the *unconventional prosperity tools* of this chapter that you may consider using to enhance your *Midas Touch*. Do not hesitate to include any unconventional techniques not discussed here.

_____

_____

_____

_____

_____

_____

_____

_____

_____

_____

Note: I must point out that *all of the above prosperity tools can only produce results when used in conjunction with other income-generating activities.* Besides using your *prosperity tools*, you still have to work in your business, or apply for a new job, or take your chances in stock trading, or do anything else related to your *Midas Touch* in order to make money. Yet, in many instances your *Midas Touch* will not work unless you apply some of these *unconventional prosperity tools.* Changing your name, re-arranging your house by Feng Shui principles, cleaning your garage, or donating money to your favorite charity can open for you the channels of prosperity, but you will need other activities to move money through these channels.

Part IV

PSYCHOLOGY OF MONEY

CHAPTER FIFTEEN

Financial Psychotherapy

Don't Trouble Trouble

So far, our discussion of the *Midas Touch* has been based on two presuppositions. One, some of the financial strategies of your family of origin are functional and can be useful for you. Two, some of the financial strategies that you have applied in the past are functional, and at least one of them can become your *Midas Touch*.

To apply the strategies discussed in Chapters Six through Fourteen, you did not have to face your unresolved psychological issues. The *Midas Touch* is the road of least resistance, where such issues do not necessarily prevent you from achieving prosperity. In some instances "psychological imperfection" may even become an important component of your *Midas Touch* strategy. We all have encountered a number of financially successful individuals who owe their fortune to their psychological imperfections. Many successful public speakers, entertainers, politicians and even government leaders exhibit the textbook features of a Narcissistic Personality Disorder. Alexander the Great and Napoleon, for example, had obvious psychological issues around their relationships with their parents. Many of Alexander's achievements sprang from his desire to outperform his father, while Napoleon's drive to conquer the world was fueled by his need to impress his mother. Most likely, without their character defects many of these narcissists would not have accomplished anything above mediocrity.

You may have found by now at least a few successful finan-cial strategies that have come to you as the result of parental con-ditioning. Trained as a psychotherapist, I can never advise you to simply continue living under the spell of parental condi-tioning. Nevertheless, I will suggest that you *consciously* use the portion of your parental conditioning that includes these successful financial strategies (either in their original or modi-fied form) as your *Midas Touch*.

In most instances, there is no need to specifically focus on resolving your psychological issues to achieve prosperity. In some cases however, these issues' resolution is paramount in order to discover and apply your *Midas Touch*.

Psychological Issues

Psychological issues are hard to define, even though the term is frequently used by mental health professionals and lay people alike. No one, even brain surgeons, has ever seen these mysterious issues. Unfortunately, not only do they exist, they may also significantly influence, occasionally even control, our lives.

I have never come across any definition of psychological issues. Therefore, I will broadly define them as various impulses, cravings and desires that cause psychological problems result-ing in dysfunctional life coping skills, faulty thinking, inappro-priate emotional responses, delusions and, in extreme cases, addictions and mental disorders.

Usually, you do not have to specifically deal with psycho-logical issues to substantially increase your income. A certain degree of resolution of some of your issues may happen indi-rectly in the process of applying your *Midas Touch*. In many instances you may be able to avoid dealing with psychological issues, since on the road to prosperity you may simply grow out of them.

In some instances however, your *Midas Touch* may be

buried under the heavy weight of your psychological issues, and you may have to resolve some of them first to uncover your *Midas Touch*. Thus, the resolution of your psychological issues becomes one of your most important tools to achieve prosperity.

So, do you have to specifically focus on your issues to acquire wealth or can you ignore them altogether? Let's figure out which is your case.

Trouble Trouble

Unfortunately, in a great many instances you will not be able to find any successful financial strategy either in your family of origin or in your experience, that would even remotely qualify for a *Midas Touch*. Frequently, your family of origin financial history, as well as your own, may have been an endless account of working hard for meager wages, or even of persistent financial failures. Here, you will not be able to use much of your family's financial strategies, since such strategies have not produced the desired results either in your life or in the life of your family of origin.

Do not despair if the above is your case. Your *Midas Touch* is still there, hidden behind your psychological issues. You may have to resolve some of these issues first to liberate your *Midas Touch*. Thus, struggling with your psychological issues becomes paramount to wealth acquisition.

Psychotherapy as Midas Touch

Psychotherapy is one of the best ways to resolve psychological issues in our modern age. Expensive as it appears, psychotherapy may help its recipients to achieve significant financial results. Psychotherapy, *if successful*, will remove obstacles on your road to prosperity, while expanding your horizon and liberating the powerful creative forces of your psyche, thus significantly increasing your income potential.

Unrecognized Desire

It is not fully recognized even in Maslow's hierarchy of needs that the desire for the resolution of psychological issues is one of the most fundamental human drives, next to survival, thirst, hunger and procreation. This may explain why we often unconsciously attract or are attracted to certain people as bosses, co-workers, customers, clients and patients with whom we re-create in our jobs or businesses the relationship similar to those we had with our parents and siblings. This provides us with an opportunity to face the issues that originated in early childhood and therefore achieve freedom from parental conditioning.

In some individuals, this desire is so overwhelming that they have to satisfy it first, before they are able to attend to their major life projects. There are also individuals for whom psychotherapy is a life mission. They either become lifetime consumers of counseling services or enter the field of the professionals providing such services. If this is your case, psychotherapy is likely to become the major component of your *Midas Touch*.

Financial Psychotherapy

Financial psychotherapy is a new emerging field and there are very few professionals that can truly call themselves financial psychotherapists. Only a very small percentage of psychotherapists incorporate financial psychotherapy into their practice. However, even these psychotherapists rarely treat financial issues as the main goal of therapy, focusing instead on psychological dysfunctions resulting from personality and psychotic disorders, or from marital discord.

Even though qualified financial psychotherapists are hard to find, this emerging field is already well represented in numerous books, articles, television programs and public seminars.

As the result of the present state of affairs, *financial psy-*

chotherapy may not differ much from any other form of psychotherapy, except that it will be focused on issues related to money.

In addition to psychotherapists, there are also a few financial planners, accountants and even lawyers who go beyond the limits of their field and attempt to help their clients with psychological issues related to money. Some of them team up with psychotherapists to create a multidisciplinary approach to such issues.

If It's Working, Don't Fix It

Financial psychotherapy may also be useful for individuals who are not willing to leave their jobs, change careers, start new businesses, reconcile with their estranged parents or initiate any drastic changes that may be required to implement their *Midas Touch*. They can still significantly improve their income from their present jobs or businesses by resolving some of their psychological issues related to money, as discussed in this chapter.

Choosing a Therapist

Psychotherapy requires time, effort and money. In the age of HMOs, we have a buyer's market in psychotherapy. Many would be willing to help you deal with your issues, but very few will be truly able to provide financial psychotherapy.

Financial psychotherapy is a fairly new phenomenon, not represented in most psychology school curricula. Therefore, your psychotherapist's degrees, license, training or theoretical orientation are of minor importance. Years of experience do not matter either, unless this experience was acquired in the field of financial psychotherapy, which is rare. *The most crucial aspect of any psychotherapy, including financial, is the rapport between you and your therapist*. It also crucial that you take charge of your own therapy and critically evaluate its results.

Taking Charge of Your Therapy

You can significantly increase the efficiency of your psychotherapy if you share with your therapist the list of your money-metaphors and the list of your cultural, personal and family myths about money that you will discover in Chapters Seventeen and Eighteen. It is especially important to inform your therapist about your family's successful and faulty financial strategies, as well as about your own financial successes and failures. Give your therapist the above information in the beginning of therapy. Otherwise, it may take months, frequently a year or more, for your therapist to discover this information on his or her own.

Taking charge of your therapy usually means that you cannot be a passive recipient of psychotherapeutic services. Instead, you and your therapist become partners equally responsible for your success. Your responsibilities include presenting your issues and setting the therapy goals, while your therapist provides the structure for resolving these issues and achieving your goals. *In financial psychotherapy, a therapist acts as a coach or a consultant, and whatever you learn in therapy you have to practice in your everyday life.*

It is also your responsibility to evaluate the progress you are making and fire your therapist, if your psychotherapy does not work. If receiving psychotherapy is an integral part of your *Midas Touch,* you will experience the *beginner's luck* phenomenon, and a couple of months of therapy will produce at least some changes in your ability to earn a living, or, even better, some income increase. If this does not happen then you have to either change your therapist or apply some other methodology to increase your income.

Preparing for Financial Psychotherapy

If you believe that financial psychotherapy is one of your options, I suggest that you prepare for your therapist all the information on your money-metaphors that you will hopefully compile at the end of Chapter Seventeen. Bring also the list of your money-myths from Chapter Eighteen, the list your family's successful and faulty financial strategies compiled in Chapters Six through Nine, and the description of the roles that you played in your family system from Chapter Eight. Add to it the lists of your financially functional as well as financially dysfunctional behaviors from the next sections of this chapter and the lists of your own successful and faulty financial strategies from Chapter Twenty-Two.

Compile the above information neatly and concisely and present it to your therapist. This will save you time and money.

Finally, keep it in mind that the self-help strategies discussed in Chapter Nineteen may become valuable additions to your therapy, also saving you time and money.

Changing Dysfunctional Behaviors

Usually, it is fairly easy to identify at least some of your dysfunctional behaviors that result in your financial limitations. Many of these behaviors can be traced to your family's faulty financial strategies, as discussed in the following case.

Case study: Mira

Mira's mother was a legendary cook. From early childhood she participated in extended family gatherings in her parents home. When she married and started her own family, she reproduced such gatherings in her own home. Relatives, friends and strangers alike flocked under her wings to satisfy their gastronomic as well as emotional needs. Mira's mother was a great giver, but she had no clue about how to receive. All attempts by her relatives and friends to reciprocate the favors were discouraged, and all her frequent guests were trained to be forever on the receiving end of her unlimited generosity. Dysfunctional as it may appear, this life strategy worked for the mother, giving her a purpose in her retirement and always placing her in a position of power and control.

When Mira became a licensed psychotherapist, she unconsciously applied her mother's strategy in her relationships with her clients. She was warm, giving, supportive, encouraging, providing numerous free services and always going an extra mile for her clients. Fortunately, in spite of her mother's frequent advice to serve food to her clients, Mira resisted her natural impulses to do so due to her fears of violating ethical standards of her profession and losing her license as a result.

Mira was a "rescuer," a psychological term for a mental health practitioner who fosters dependency relationships with clients. Unfortunately, her mother's life coping skills did not work for Mira financially. She had a hard time charging for her counseling services and unconsciously even encouraged her clients not to pay. Even though Mira was qualified as a therapist, in some areas even exceptional, her problems with charging the appropriate fees brought her to close to financial ruin. We have already discussed in Chapter Three how she resolved her issues indirectly by hiring interns and a secretary responsible for billing and fee collection.

* * *

Hopefully, you can identify by now the specific repertoire of behaviors that have not been working for you in money matters. Usually, such behaviors can be traced to your family's faulty financial strategies as illustrated above. Occasionally, your financially dysfunctional behaviors may have no identifiable sources, but they still interfere with your life just the same. List these financially dysfunctional behaviors, learned from your family of origin or developed on your own.

Financially Dysfunctional Behaviors

_____

_____

_____

_____

_____

_____

_____

_____

_____

_____

Financially Functional Behaviors

You may have discovered by now the financially functional behaviors that can replace your financially dysfunctional ones listed above. List these functional behaviors below.

_____

_____

_____

_____

_____

_____

_____

_____

_____

Do not be disturbed by having difficulties compiling this list. You may need more time to think about it, or to ask for help from your friends or your therapist.

The realization that some of your behaviors are financially dysfunctional rarely stops you from employing them. There is often a great distance between being aware of your dysfunctional behaviors and changing or eliminating them. It is difficult, for some people impossible, to change such behaviors without outside help. In this case, financial psychotherapy might be particularly indicated. If you are really short on funds and cannot afford psychotherapy, enlist your friends' help in changing your financially dysfunctional behaviors. Some of the strategies discussed in the following chapters, such as affirmations, visualization and prayer, may also bring the desirable behavioral changes.

CHAPTER SIXTEEN

Family Therapy

The financial psychotherapy discussed above is based on the presupposition that the psychological issues causing your faulty financial strategies concern you only, and can be dealt with in your individual therapy. However, if you have a family of your own, or at least a significant other, another dimension is added to your life. In this case, in order to deal with the issues related to money, family therapy may be recommended.

Family therapy is based on systems theory. One of the basic principles of family therapy is that every family, even a family of two unmarried individuals living together, is a system that must maintain balance between its parts in order to exist. Every family employs various psychological mechanisms to stay in balance. If one of the family members undergoes a change, and every change disturbs the system's balance, the other family members respond by trying to prevent or at least limit this change in order to maintain the system's equilibrium. Thus, if your significant other attempts to resolve his or her issues related to money and begins to earn more, you may be compelled to resist or sabotage his or her effort. Such actions directed to maintaining the family equilibrium are usually, but not always, unconscious. You may unconsciously resist your partner's progress in spite of your sincere desire for him or her to succeed.

Lust for Power

This curious and not especially attractive remnant of our primitive instinctual drives still operates in many relationships, including the modern family system. The fact that this lust for power is purely instinctual does not make it any less potent. No matter how educated, emancipated and benevolent both you and your partner are, the power struggle in your dyad is unavoidable, and many issues in this power struggle may revolve around money. The partner earning more money generally has an advantage in winning this struggle and gaining many real or perceived advantages which power and control may bring. Unfortunately, this power struggle has no real winners. Regardless of the outcome, both combatants lose.

Here are a few strategies, which you or your partner may consciously or unconsciously apply in this power struggle, and which you and your partner may have to avoid.

Demoralization

Suppose your partner acts as a critical parent. Such a partner would constantly criticize your shortcomings, including your inability to bring home sufficient income. Occasionally, such partners may apply quite dubious, vicious and psychologically sophisticated strategies to demoralize you, and often they succeed. A demoralized partner does not pose a threat, is less likely to be sexually attractive to others, and has little chance to make more money. In extreme cases, they have no chance to make money at all.

Double Messages

In relationships, every action is a communication. Thus, if you demand that your partner begins to earn a living, and at the same time lavish him or her with expensive gifts, or pay for the partner's housing, food, clothes, entertainment and medical care, your actions are incongruent with your words. Here, your double message is confusing, keeping your partner from moving towards financial independence. However, such incongruent communication may enable you to better control your partner.

Sabotage

Case study: Pamela and Carl

Pamela, a young attractive 30-year old divorcee, had no place to live and no skill to make it in the world. So, instead of struggling with issues of jobs and money, she moved in with Carl, who adored her. Pamela did not care about Carl, but he owned a house and had some savings that provided them both with a meager existence. In spite of the lack of reciprocity, the relationship was stable without any apparent major problems until Carl began to apply for high-paying jobs to improve their financial situation. Pamela, terrified that this change might raise her partner's self-esteem and bring him in contact with other women who could find him attractive, actively sabotaged his efforts to get a job. Her favorite strategy was to initiate verbal confrontations with crying and screaming right before Carl's important job interviews. She usually succeeded in either making him late for the interviews or getting him so upset that he could not conduct such interviews well enough to get selected for a job. For months, she was winning the power struggle by successfully sabotaging Carl's efforts. Unfortunately, any power struggle has no winners. Even though Carl loved Pamela, he could not endure her sabotaging behavior for long. Eventually, this relationship was terminated.

Pamela's sabotage is not a typical example. Commonly, such sabotage is a lot more subtle, and rarely results in the relationship termination. However, it maintains the status quo in the family power struggle, while preventing either or both partners from achieving financial success.

Dysfunctional Strategies of Power Struggle

Besides the three strategies discussed above, there are many others that you or your partner may apply to each other with unfortunate consequences for the family's income. So, in the blank spaces below, write down a list of them. If you are aware of any such strategy in your or your partner's family, also include them here.

Yours

_____
_____
_____
_____
_____
_____
_____
_____
_____
_____

Your Partner's

_____
_____
_____
_____
_____
_____
_____
_____
_____
_____

The above list may be treated the same way as the dysfunctional behaviors discussed in the previous chapter. Changing such behaviors without a qualified marriage counselor may be difficult, if not impossible. If you choose to consult such a counselor, showing him or her the above list from the start may speed up your therapy and increase your chances for success.

CHAPTER SEVENTEEN

Money as a Metaphor

The strategies presented in Chapters Six through Fourteen are based on common sense, and have been commonly used in our culture for a few hundred years. These commonsensical solutions do not challenge any of the traditional beliefs about money. Nor do they require you to drastically alter your lifestyle. Unfortunately, these strategies do not work for all. For some, it becomes necessary to re-examine and change their beliefs and values, as well as significantly alter their thinking process, to achieve their financial goals. If this is your case, you may have to learn about money metaphors, discussed in this chapter. These metaphors influence the way you think about money and therefore frequently determine your financial successes or failures.

This chapter, as well the following one, may appear a bit too philosophical for some of my readers. If this is true for you, skip both of them and go to Chapter Nineteen.

The Power of Metaphors

The role of metaphors in our life is highly underrated. They are typically viewed as mere poetic and imaginative expressions of language. Yet, besides serving as the means for communication, they also play a central role in the construction of our social and political reality. The power of metaphors is immense, and there is probably no aspect of our existence where metaphors do not influence or even rule our life. *Metaphors also rule our monetary exchange and greatly influence, at times even determine, our financial success or failure.* So, let's examine these metaphors at closer range.

Associations

Our language is rich with abstract concepts that are difficult to define. Often, the only way to communicate such concepts is by their associations with other concepts related to them that are commonly used in everyday life. Thus throughout history, gold has been associated with such abstract concepts as personal safety, social status, professional competence, popularity, power, self-esteem, freedom, love and happiness. A couple of centuries ago, such associations were transferred to paper money, so we may say that money, paper or coin, has become a metaphor for all these intangible concepts mentioned above.

Money metaphors are not the only metaphors that we use. There are thousands of others that we frequently encounter in our language. Here are a few examples taken (with some modification) from G. Lakoff's and M. Johnson's *Metaphors We Live By:*

TIME IS MONEY
You are wasting your time.
How do you spend your time?
I have invested a lot of time in this project.

ARGUMENT IS WAR
He attacked every point in my arguments.
Your point of view is indefensible.
I never won an argument with my wife.

The Definition of a Metaphor

The dictionary defines a metaphor as a figure of speech in which one object is likened to another by speaking of it as if it were another object. In literature, especially in poetry, as well as in conversational language, metaphors help to define, clarify or stress various points we are trying to make, or express various subtle meanings and undertones of our communication.

Metaphors and Perception of Reality

Once created and frequently used in language, metaphors acquire the power of their own to mold our thinking, attitudes, emotional responses and eventually our actions. If a metaphor is introduced into our language and into our consciousness, it has the power to influence how we perceive reality. This metaphor becomes a self-fulfilling prophecy by significantly influencing the course of our life events, as well as providing a conceptual framework for their understanding. An example of such a metaphor is provided below.

Money as a Metaphor for Survival

At the time of this writing, the average one-bedroom apartment rents for $600-1,200 a month in many metropolitan areas of the U.S. Usually, it takes one person about three times as much—$2,000-3,000 a month—to just "survive." You obviously noticed that I am using quotation marks for the word "survive." However, once this word got associated with money, it has become a metaphor for survival. It appears that the word survive has lost its quotation marks, and most of us now truly believe that it takes at least $2,000 a month just to survive. Our subconscious makes us forget that it is not our survival at stake here, but our ability to maintain the middle class lifestyle to which we got accustomed to since childhood. In reality, you will not die if your income falls below this magic number of

$2,000 a month, or even below $1,000, or even if it goes to zero. You may become very unhappy living on such income, perhaps even homeless, but you will survive. Obviously, you and your family will not surely die on the reduced income.

Metaphors Measure Reality

How do we measure security, well-being, social status, professional competence and many other abstract and intangible objects? Since all these things are psychological constructs and have only relative existence, they can only be measured indirectly through their metaphors. Thus, the type of car that one drives, the house that one owns or clothes that one wears can be used to measure, though often inadequately, one's professional competence, social status or personal safety. Unfortunately, most people evaluate us by our status symbols, rather than through personal interaction.

Money as a Means of Exchange

Money is real, even though a few daring souls attempt, usually unsuccessfully, to deny its existence. Originally, money was used mostly for the exchange of daily necessities, like food, clothes, agricultural tools, kitchen utensils, domestic animals, land, weapons and medical treatment. So, already in antiquity money became a metaphor, a symbolic and arbitrary representation of a unit of labor required to produce a symbolic unit of basic human needs. Even then, mankind had to deal with wild currency fluctuations, since the symbolic meaning of money would vary depending on the moods of the populace and the desires of its rulers.

Distorted Mirrors

Money metaphors are like distorted mirrors in a fun house. Such mirrors make us laugh because they distort reality. There is always a real object reflected in such a mirror, frequently distorted to the point of no recognition. Thus fat people may appear there as skinny, or short people as tall.

Distorted mirrors are fun, but can you imagine taking what you see there on face value? Probably not. However, most of us do take the money metaphors, distortions as they may be, as accurate reflections of reality. Needless to say that we do so unconsciously as a result of our cultural conditioning. Frequently, we also create a few of our own metaphors adding to that distortion.

If you want to achieve prosperity it is crucial to become a master of your own money metaphors. The first step toward this mastery is the realization that *money is only a metaphor for things, like food, clothes or shelter, but it can never become those things. Money can be used as a measure of self-esteem, success, love, security, power, control, etc., but it can never become those intangible psychological constructs.*

In fact, money is frequently not even a good metaphor for the things, tangible or intangible, that it is supposed to stand for. For example, we believe that our happiness and well-being depends on the amount of money we make. So, more money will reflect greater happiness. In many instances however, money does not reflect happiness. Some of us are so dedicated to financial success that we sacrifice everything to it, thus becoming miserable in the process of wealth acquisition. Here, more money does not reflect happiness, it reflects misery instead.

At times, when money is supposed to measure love, it may only measure indifference, or an illusion of love instead. Often, money that is supposed to be a measure of security, is really only an illusion of this security. So, let's examine some of the most common money metaphors, and discover how accurately they stand for things tangible and intangible that they are supposed to represent.

Money as a Metaphor for Love

Early in childhood, we learn to associate money with love and care. Our parents' little treats, such as toys, candies, ice-cream, merry-go-round, etc., made money a metaphor for love. (Occasionally these "little" gifts may cost a fortune and become a major family expense.) In addition, our parents fed, clothed, sheltered and educated us, which required money, and a lot of it. Naturally, as adults we associate money with the ability to love and care, and there is some truth in this. However, in numerous instances money can also be a substitute for love, and lead to some popular delusions, as illustrated by the following examples.

Case study: The woman with nine credit cards

This case is taken from David Wallin's audio book, *Money Matters in Psychotherapy,* which presents a woman who lived lavishly and extravagantly. She was buying on whim whatever her heart desired, using her nine credit cards. She had no intention of paying back her credit card debts. In her mind, the credit card companies were a metaphor for her parents, still bestowing her with gifts and taking care of all her needs and whims. Credit card spending became her metaphor for unconditional love.

This woman's delusion is shared by many. Many Americans owe thousands of dollars in credit card debt. Some have owed so much that they have very little chance of ever paying it back.

Case study: Sara

Sara, a small business owner, also used money as a metaphor for love by going on shopping sprees. When feeling stressed out by the demands of her business, she discovered that shopping allowed her to regress to the carefree life of her childhood, when her all-powerful and wealthy father used to take her shopping, buying her anything that she asked for.

Unfortunately, Sara is not unusual in her shopping sprees. There are so many like her that we may say that America has become a nation of "shopoholics," and millions around the globe share Sara's obsession as well.

Money as a Metaphor for Dependency

Case study: Arnold

Arnold is a 30-year-old artist, still living at home. He never made any money from his art, and never even tried. Arnold occasionally works part-time doing various non-demanding jobs while earning minimal wages. The money that he earns is nowhere near enough to pay his bills. Arnold feels miserable. He would like to live a normal life. To him, as to most people of his age, this means having his own place and making enough money to pay his bills. He would also like to have friends and form romantic relationships. At present he has none. There is nothing wrong with Arnold, physically or intellectually. He is simply afraid to face this dangerous and hostile world, and prefers the security and comfort of his mother's home. For Arnold, money, or the lack of it, became a metaphor of his dependency on his mother. The money metaphor of dependency is shared by his mother as well. A middle-aged divorcee, with the rest of her children grown and gone, she is scared to live alone in her huge house, so she actively maintains her son's dependency on her.

Money as a Metaphor for Power

The use of money as a metaphor for power is so widespread and so common that it does not require any additional explanations or examples. Indeed, in many instances money does measure one's ability to have power and control over others. However, the expanse of this power given by money is frequently greatly exaggerated. In most instances, money alone will not buy much influence, status and prestige, unless one finds access to the appropriate social circles.

Money as a Metaphor for Freedom

The use of money as a metaphor for freedom is also common. Most believe that with more money they will achieve greater freedom to do whatever they want. In many instances, money indeed equals freedom, but this freedom is never unlimited. For some, who spend a great portion of their life enduring semi-feudal conditions working 9 to 5 plus overtime and a long commute, the process of making money actually limits their personal freedom to weekends and brief vacations. Besides, having money brings additional responsibilities, as illustrated by the following case.

Case study: Mohammed

Mohammed, a computer store owner, emigrated from Pakistan twelve years ago. In his first years in America, his income was very modest, but he always sent a portion of it to his family in Pakistan. Mohammed was talented, hard working and lucky. Soon his business was earning big profits, and Mohammed was able to send his family larger amounts of money. As his business grew, so grew the financial needs of two of his brothers and a sister back home. His siblings were all grown adults, all married with children, and none of them or their spouses or children were employed. Mohammed ended up financially supporting more than a dozen people, who had no intention of ever getting a job. Sometimes he jokes that he may return to Pakistan and run for a political office there. This would give him a chance to improve Pakistan's economy, so that his siblings could not use the bad economy as an excuse for their financial dependency. Thus, Mohammed's financial success

191

in America did not liberate him. It increased his responsibilities instead.

Unfortunately, Mohammed's case is not unusual. There are too many like him for whom an income increase brings additional burdens.

Money as a Metaphor for Self-Esteem

The use of money as a metaphor for self-esteem is closely related to its use as a metaphor for power. In many instances, greater income does produce greater self-esteem. Just as frequently however, it produces only "the horse running after the carrot" phenomenon. Many chase after money to increase their sense of self-worth, only to discover that it cannot be based entirely upon wealth.

Money as a Metaphor for Submission

As children, many may have learned that their parents preferred an obedient child to a talented one, and the exhibition of any special qualities or strength of character could make parents uncomfortable. Usually, siblings and peers also prefer an ordinary companion whom they can control rather than a rival with whom they have to compete. As a consequence, some learn to cultivate mediocrity in order to fit in. Besides, parents, teachers, siblings and friends often place higher demands on the talented and unique, so some children "become ordinary" to avoid conflicts and responsibilities. As an adult, such a person, no matter how talented, will always exercise his or her skills to never earn more than his or her parents, siblings, friends and associates. Such a person may not become a complete failure, but neither will he or she experience success. For such individuals, money is a metaphor for submission and acceptance.

Money as a Metaphor for Parenting

Parents frequently sacrifice their lives for their children, working at jobs which they do not like and which damage their physical and mental health. They do this to provide the children with the very best, which usually costs a lot of money. For such parents, money has become a metaphor for good parenting. Only a few realize that such sacrifices are frequently not only useless, but occasionally can be harmful. Overworked, tired and frustrated parents may not be able to adequately take care of their kids. Furthermore, since parents are their children's primary role models, children learn (absorb would be a better word) their parents' life coping skills. Therefore, children raised by unhappy parents who sacrifice their life for their children's sake are likely to grow up into unhappy adults, sacrificing their life for their children as well. Thus, the practice of sacrificing one's life for the children may continue indefinitely through generations.

Do you want to teach your children how to endure suffering, or how to become a well-balanced and happy adult? Either way, your children will learn by your example.

What Are Your Money Metaphors?

Here is your chance to examine your own money metaphors. Which of the metaphors discussed above apply to you? Are there any other money metaphors in your life that were not mentioned in this book? Fill in the empty spaces below with your own money metaphors.

_____

_____

_____

_____

_____

_____

Money as an Evolutionary Force

The use of money as a metaphor for a great many things is not only useful, but will occasionally produce astounding results. Indeed, money as a metaphor for success and personal glory has encouraged many heroic deeds. Explorers, inventors, artists, politicians, military heroes, and countless remarkable people from all fields of human endeavor were motivated at least partially by money metaphors, meaning the value that they assigned to money. Many of them would have never accomplished anything without their attachment to such money metaphors, and humanity would still be living in the Dark Ages as a result.

Metaphors Be with You

Together with Mr. Spock's "Live long and prosper" from *Star Trek* and Clint Eastwood's "Go ahead, make my day" from *Dirty Harry*, "May the force be with you" from *Star Wars* is one of the most remembered and widely used phrases of modern cinematography. Curiously, "May the force be with you" is phonetically almost identical to "Metaphors be with you." Perhaps, the nearly identical pronunciation of these two phrases hints at the kinship of the force of *Star Wars* with the psychological force of metaphors, including the metaphors of money. Like the force, psychological metaphors are almost all powerful. Like the force, such metaphors must be controlled. Otherwise, the metaphors become like the dark side of the force from *Star Wars* and take control of you. Therefore, ***Metaphors be with you, not against you!***

CHAPTER EIGHTEEN

Cultural Myths

Financial success or failure is frequently associated with myths that many have accepted as true. Such myths, most of which have nothing to do with reality, were ingrained into our subconscious in early childhood. Some of these myths may be still buried in your subconscious, creating a complex web of dysfunctional behaviors, faulty concepts, justifications and delusions that may interfere with your ability to generate income.

Fortunately, most of us do not have to thoroughly examine and completely eradicate all such myths from our subconscious. Millions of very imperfect and highly dysfunctional individuals, in spite of having "bought into" various cultural myths, are still able to generate substantial income. Chances are that you do not have to struggle with the cultural myths that are responsible for some of your negative beliefs. Instead, you can ignore, avoid or—even better—use them to your advantage.

However, it is also possible that you belong to a sizable minority, for whom financial success is impossible without shattering at least some of your cultural, family and personal myths.

Let's examine some of these myths related to success, prosperity and money, and figure out how they may be affecting your life.

"Happiness for the Strong, Sorrow for the Weak."

"Happiness for the strong, sorrow for the weak" is the title of a popular Russian folk song that states that only exceptional individuals can achieve success and happiness in life. The rest must accept their fate and give up trying to rise above their meager existence. This song provides a typically Russian solution to dealing with human sorrow: drinking oneself to oblivion.

Fortunately for us, the notion that happiness and prosperity are only for the exceptionally gifted and superior is not true. Just glancing through history books and looking around you, you can easily discover that the multitudes of creative geniuses with exceptional strength of character and with truly superhuman qualities died in poverty or perished in a thousand different ways. History books and local newspapers will also inform you that most of the rich, famous, powerful and successful of all times, including the present, were as ordinary and highly imperfect human beings as you and I. In fact, many of them were a lot more dysfunctional than us, as history has testified.

You have also observed that numerous quite ordinary individuals with no superhuman qualities have still achieved extraordinary financial success.

So, you do not necessarily have to be special or superior in anything to be rich.

Only the Intelligent Can Achieve Prosperity

This statement is partially true. Indeed, many, but not all, financially successful people seem to exhibit above average intelligence. However, a lot of highly intelligent people are not especially successful financially, some live in poverty, and a few are homeless. You do not need above average intelligence to realize that *intelligence by itself does not guarantee financial success.*

Prosperity is Only for the Educated

According to statistics, the well educated earn a lot more than the rest, and many financially successful people are well educated. However, a lot of very educated individuals encounter financial difficulties as often than their uneducated brethren, and a few are homeless and destitute.

In fact, *an individual's academic achievement correlates with his or her talents and skills in abstract thinking, while financial success usually requires an adequate development in concrete and practical thinking, which will always include relationship skills.* The absent-minded professor, one of the popular characters of our comic stories, illustrates that talents and skills in academia may not be transferable to one's success in everyday life. Education or intelligence may even be a hindrance to financial success. Many highly educated and intelligent people prefer to dwell in the world of ideas, where they feel at home. Such individuals create a complex web of intellectualizations and justifications to avoid the pain of confronting their ineptitude at living in our quite concrete world and financially succeeding in it.

On the other hand, a few school dropouts, like Anthony Robbins, the success coach and author, become exceptionally rich. Therefore, we do not need above-average education to realize that *education by itself does not determine financial success.*

The Myth of Psychological Perfection

Some believe that financial success can only be achieved by well-adjusted individuals from fully functional families (if such a thing exists) who do not struggle with psychological issues like the rest of us. But what about countless examples like this:

Case study: Morris

Morris and his wife arrived in the U.S. in their twenties. They were both holocaust survivors. Like many others who experienced the horror of Hitler's concentration camps, they developed various psychological problems, such as anxiety and insomnia.

Healthy or not, you have to make money in order to live. So, Morris and his wife opened a small coffee shop in downtown San Francisco. There, they both worked all their lives from dawn to dusk seven days a week, including weekends and holidays. They did not mind such a work schedule since it allowed them to escape their painful memories.

Eventually, Morris and his wife became exceptionally wealthy, but derived very little pleasure from their financial success. They did have a beautiful house, and were able to send their daughter to a prestigious school, but their life was still void of fun, entertainment or any pleasure whatsoever. For several decades, there was no break in their boring monotonous work. Only in their sixties, did they take their first vacation. Unfortunately, they could not enjoy it, since by that time they had developed marital problems eventually leading to a painful divorce.

I definitely do not advise using Morris as a role model. However, his case illustrates that *you do not need to be psychologically perfect to achieve financial success.*

Prosperity Is Only for the Righteous

At the dawn of history, humankind developed various moral codes of behaviors designed to appease the gods and inspire the immortals to bestow upon their faithful devotees various blessings, which usually included prosperity. As religions rose and fell, those codes kept changing, frequently losing their religious significance when the culture became more secular. One thing remained the same. At any historical period, there was a great number of individuals who strictly followed the moral code of their time, and still lived a miserable life, while some of their contemporaries ignored most of the moral restrictions, but prospered nevertheless.

A prominent Jewish Sage, Rabbi Akiva, said, "Suffering of the righteous and prosperity of the wicked is one of God's mysteries."

It appears that *following high moral principles is not enough to achieve prosperity.*

Only the Wicked Prosper

Very few people believe in this myth anymore, and those who do, use it to justify their financial failures. I am not aware of any statistical research focused on the correlation between one's moral development and one's financial success. Nevertheless, it is obvious that in all social circles, there appears to be no such correlation at all. Therefore, *lack of moral principles will not necessarily make you rich.*

"By the Sweat of Thy Brow"

"By the sweat of thy brow, you will eat your daily bread" is one of the oldest myths. When translated into modern language, it means that only by working very hard can you pay your bills. This myth is a vast generalization that does not apply in many cases. You can easily find numerous individuals working harder than you do, and still unable to make ends meet; as well as many who do nothing at all and still live in riches.

Hard work is not a guarantor of financial success.

Going the Extra Mile

My parents taught me that doing favors for people will inspire them to reciprocate such favors. Later on, I met many people like myself who would respond way beyond the call of duty by helping others. All these naive individuals, myself included, expected good treatment and favors in return. We were wrong, and here is why:

As a rule, animals do not reciprocate favors. Once fed or taken care of in any meaningful way, such biological beings are likely to come back for more, instead of doing something in return for you. Thus, if you feed a dog, it may come back to you when hungry. If you feed it repeatedly, this dog may get attached to you, but do not expect it to feed you in return. Yes, the dog will guard your house. In doing so, it will not reciprocate your favors, but follow its instincts instead.

At this stage of our social development, many human beings would respond to your favors in the manner of the dog described above: you feed them or take care of them, and they come back for more. This quality of human nature to always hope for a "free lunch" is used in department store sales, direct mail promotions, etc., that advertise free or very cheap products and services to lure customers to the store, but we all know that there are always hooks attached.

Naturally, you will find many people who would gladly reciprocate favors and who would go an extra mile for you. However, reciprocity is not yet an integral part of human behavior. In some cultures, it is an exception rather than the rule.

Unless you are surrounded by highly evolved people, *going an extra mile or doing beyond the call of duty cannot guarantee your success.*

Prosperity Pill

We have already discussed this matter in Chapter One. However, this myth has so many ardent believers that it would be useful to repeat a few points here.

Unfortunately, no such magic pill will ever be produced, and all the systems of prosperity presented by the most brilliant minds will *not* work for the vast majority of the population.

Such methodologies of prosperity can only work for those who created them and for a few of their followers, but they are not appropriate for most of us. We all are different in our backgrounds, talents, abilities, strengths, weaknesses, personal preferences, etc. *A methodology of prosperity that would fit us all will never be found.*

Religion and Spirituality

The myth that living in poverty is a must for a spiritual and religious life does not correlate with reality. I did not find aversion to money or riches in the written biographies of the founders of the major world religions. According to the Bible, Abraham was a prosperous man, and Moses experienced no deprivation, except during his solo journey in the desert. Some of Jesus' statements criticizing the rich are recorded in the Four Gospels. However, even the Apostles did not interpret such statements as instructions to be poor, since some of the original Christian churches became rich. The founder of Islam, Mohammed acquired wealth through marriage. The founder of Buddhism, Prince Siddharta lived an ascetic life. Yet, he accepted large donations to support his army of monks. Looking through history, I could not find a definite correlation between spirituality and financial success or failure. It appears that highly evolved souls simply do not care about money, as they are often indifferent to comfort, sex, entertainment and most of the things dear to you and me. They are indifferent, but not antagonistic. Therefore, *poverty has no correlation with spirituality, and spirituality is not in conflict with wealth.*

Cultural, Family and Personal Myths

Besides the most common myths presented above, there are also myths that are spread only within a specific nationality, or within a certain social class. There are also myths common in certain geographical locations, those shared only by members of the same family, and finally there are personal myths that exist only inside one's own mind. All such myths are generalizations, for which the opposite may be equally true. Therefore, they are half-truths at best. Mythology, an important part of our culture, may become useful if you look at it from a historical perspective. However, taking myths about money literally may not only prevent your financial success, but may also lead you to your financial demise.

Here is your chance to examine your own myths about money. Which of the myths discussed above do you believe in? Are there any other myths that you may have accepted as the truth, not mentioned in this book? Fill in the empty spaces below with your own myths about money. This simple exercise may help you to remove the obstacles from your path to financial freedom and will be useful for the subsequent chapters.

_____

_____

_____

_____

_____

_____

_____

_____

_____

_____

CHAPTER NINETEEN

Self-Help

A Bit of History

The financial strategies discussed here can be found in almost any self-help book. Two of them, affirmations and visualizations, belong to the most popular financial strategies ever applied, especially in the 1970s and 1980s. The enthusiasts of the human potential movement prescribed them as a fast cure for all physical, psychological and social problems, which, of course, was a gross exaggeration. Affirmations and visualizations are still popular today. The reason for their popularity is simple: they require very little effort. All you have to do is to repeat certain positive statements, called affirmations, or create pleasant images in your mind, called visualizations. Half-an-hour daily is enough to achieve significant life transformations. You do not have to change anything in your life. No actions required, no risk to take, no minimal investment. Nevertheless, success is guaranteed. Sounds like a sales pitch? Well, it is.

In the 1990s, the popularity of the human potential movement declined, but its methodologies went mainstream and got incorporated in psychology as self-help tools, and into industry and marketing as motivational tools.

Advantages and Limitations

All the strategies presented here can be used in conjunction with any other financial strategies that you may choose to apply. If they work, and frequently they do, the results can be quite dramatic, achieved with minimal effort. However, such results can only be achieved if one of these strategies is your *Midas Touch*. If it is not, then the strategies described below might be helpful, but much less than miraculous.

The Theory

There are a few theories that attempt to explain the effectiveness of self-help strategies. I prefer the one that suggests that we look at the human mind as a computer, programmed by our parents, teachers, siblings and other care providers in early childhood. Some of those programs were defective from the start, others became dysfunctional due to the change of circumstances. Most of these programs can be changed, modified or erased altogether by applying the specific self-help techniques discussed below.

Positive Thinking

This strategy would become a universal *Midas Touch*, if not for insurmountable difficulties in its implementation. Research indicates that the anxiety-producing (negative) thoughts crossing the mind of the average American every hour vastly outnumbers calming (positive) thoughts for the same period. Unfortunately, my own observations of myself and my clients confirm these findings, and many of my colleagues would make the same statement.

To change all this negativity programmed into your mind is not easy, and may require years. Nevertheless, the idea is very appealing. There are many who attempt to think positively about everything and everyone, while trying to let go of anger, hate, resentment and judgment, and expect only positive outcomes of any occurrence. Some of them have reported significant financial improvement, which they attribute to the power of positive thinking.

If this strategy is your *Midas Touch*, it should improve your financial situation in a few months. If it does not, thinking positively may still be very useful for your self-improvement, but not so in making money. Apply common sense though. Occasionally, this strategy may even lead to financial losses, since you may become overly optimistic in certain matters.

For more information on this strategy, look at *The Dynamic Laws of Prosperity* by Catherine Ponder.

Affirmations

Prosperity affirmations are phrases stating that you already have the desired wealth in the present, or that you will come to possess it by a specific future date.

Such affirmations are always positive, containing no negative words like "no, not, none, never, neither, nor."

Some affirmations can be specific, stating the exact amount of money, or other valuables, that you want to generate by a certain date. Here is a good example: *By the end of the year, my income will rise to $100,000 a year.*

Other affirmations are general, such as, *Every day in every way, I draw into my life people, events, circumstances and conditions that lead me to prosperity.*

You may use as few as two to three affirmations, or as many as twelve. None of my students were able to use successfully more than twelve affirmations at a time.

With affirmations, you may occasionally succeed in correcting some faulty financial strategies that failed you in the past. Thus, kind and compassionate Mira, who was taken advantages of by her clients (see Chapter Fifteen) could use the following affirmations: *I am a qualified, educated and experienced psychotherapist. With all my clients, I establish strictly professional relationships with strong and clear boundaries.*

Reciting your affirmations thirty minutes a day is usually enough. The best time to use them is when in bed, either right before falling sleep, or first thing upon awakening. If you fall asleep too fast, or are always in a hurry in the morning, try other times.

If you want to explore this strategy as your possible *Midas Touch,* consider reading a few good books on the subject, one of the best of them being Catherine Ponder's *The Dynamic Laws of Prosperity.*

Visualizations

Visualizations work on the same principle as affirmations, and their applications are also very similar. The main difference is that instead of using verbal statements, as in affirmations, in visualizations you use mental imagery to propel your mind into actions.

With this technique, you imagine already possessing the desired wealth in the present, or coming to possess it by the specific future date. In addition to visualizing a specific amount, you can also imagine all the desirable changes already taking place in your life as the result of the wealth that you are about to acquire. Images with strong emotional content are likely to produce greater results. As with affirmations, your mental pictures should always be positive.

You will probably achieve the best results by combining your visualizations with your affirmations, doing the affirmations first.

Visualizations may also be used to correct faulty financial strategies that failed you in the past. Thus Mira could benefit by combining her affirmation, *With all my clients, I establish strictly professional relationships with strong and clear boundaries,* with visualizing how she would actually do it with each of her clients, making it quite specific.

If visualization is indeed your *Midas Touch,* practicing it for half an hour a day will produce adequate results. Spending more time visualizing is unlikely to accelerate your progress. The best time to visualize is right before falling sleep, or first thing upon awakening. If this does not work for you, try other times.

Reading a few good books on the subject, such as Richard Bach's *Illusions* or Shakti Gawein's *Creative Visualization*, will improve your chances of succeeding with this technique.

Use of Dreams

It is better to use affirmations and visualizations before sleep because they may produce dreams about prosperity. Such dreams have occasionally caused significant positive changes for my previous students. Dreams have the power of hypnotic suggestions to restructure your psyche and unconsciously propel you toward specific actions that will bring the desired results. They may also give you specific instructions on what you have to do for wealth acquisition. In either case, record as many of your dreams as you can remember in the morning, even though many of them may not make any sense. With practice, your dreams will become more clear, and your ability to interpret them will also improve.

Consider also recording your affirmations and listening to them, while asleep. Or record a short story reflecting your visualization content and listen to it while you sleep. If this causes any sleep disturbances, discontinue this practice for a few days and restart it with a lower volume.

Specificity

Your ability to achieve results with visualizations or affirmations is likely to work in a specific field, and may not be transferable to other fields, as illustrated in the following case.

Case study: Gary

Gary was a psychology professor, who dedicated all his life to practices similar to those discussed above. He had many proven records of success in applying them for self improvement. However, he failed totally and miserably in trying to obtain money or objects of value by visualizing them. For months, he visualized a large white pearl in his palm, could see it perfectly clearly in his mind, and even feel its weight. Yet, the pearl did not materialize. Visualizing money also produced no effect. It appears that this type of visualization was not his *Midas Touch*. Perhaps, he would have done better by visualizing himself successfully implementing other financial strategies. As they say, the proof is in the pudding.

Radiating Wealth

Here you visualize that you constantly radiate wealth. For the best results, you need to apply such imagery as frequently as a few minutes every hour. You may have a hard time remembering to do so. Do not worry. It would be the case with most of us. So, give a try for a month. If this strategy is indeed your *Midas Touch,* you will succeed in it.

In addition, you may dress, speak, think, act and spend as a wealthy person. This does not mean that you can go on shopping sprees, or spend extravagantly. Shopping sprees are frequently the signs of insecurity in one's ability to sustain wealth, or a childlike attempt to grab whatever one can while the money lasts.

Attracting Wealth

Here, you visualize that you are like a magnet constantly attracting wealth, and that all people, events and conditions in your life bring you money or valuables, or lead you to prosperity. This visualization also requires a few minutes of reinforcement every hour, until it becomes automatic. It might be impossible in the beginning to find a few minutes every hour. Do the best you can. If this strategy is your *Midas Touch,* you will be able to muster it.

Self-hypnosis

Most of the techniques discussed in this chapter are more effective if you use them in altered states of consciousness. I will not get into a discussion here about altered states. There are plenty of books to get you more enlightened, or more confused, about the subject. Instead, I will suggest that you *attend a self-hypnosis class in your area to learn how to use affirmations and visualizations in trance to make them more effective.* I have been teaching such classes since 1992, and my students have found them very useful.

Collages

Besides visualization and affirmations, you can collect old magazine and newspaper clippings and create a collage that contains the images representing success to you. The act of physically cutting and pasting these pictures can intensify the intensity of your desires, thus increasing your chances to make them manifest.

The beauty of this technique is that you have to prepare such a collage only once. Then place it on your bedroom wall and look at your collage last thing before falling asleep and first thing after awakening. Your subconscious will do the rest.

Case study: Joseph

Joseph attended a seminar, called *Initiation into Success,* where he made a collage picturing what he truly wanted from life. Years passed by, and Joseph forgot all about it until he fell in love with a woman who reminded him of the picture in his collage. Then he also realized that most of the collage's content had materialized in his life over the years.

Meditation

Meditation can reduce anxiety, fear and aggression, which may produce marked improvement in your performance, as well as in your ability to relate. It can also clear the mind, enabling you to see your faulty financial strategies, as well as new opportunities to increase your income. I have observed a few instances of financial improvement in my associates resulting from their meditation practice. However, meditation will produce a substantial improvement in your income only if it is your innate *Midas Touch*. So, if after meditating for a couple of months, you do not experience marked financial improvement, meditation may still be very helpful, but do not expect it to make any difference in your financial situation.

Dress for Success

The dress for success financial strategy has been in use for thousands of years. It is so popular today that you may find 22 titles on *Amazon.com* related to the subject. Most of us are aware of the importance of dressing appropriately to achieve financial success. Yet, many totally ignore this strategy altogether to their financial detriment, as illustrated in the following case.

Case Study: Sofia

Sofia was a hairdresser. Even though she was qualified and loved her work, she struggled financially because she dressed too casually for her job. Her clients liked her work, but they discounted her as a qualified professional because she did not look the part. As a result, most of her first-time clients never came back. Needless to say that she could not attract wealthy clients with expensive tastes, who would have paid her good tips.

* * *

Going to the opposite extreme by dressing too formally, may also work to your disadvantage. You may overdress for your position, intimidating your co-workers or clients, or looking out of sync with your environment. Besides, dressing too formally may cause an inner stiffness in you, thus contributing to the tensions and anxieties that you may subconsciously broadcast to the world.

If you normally dress casually, try to dress up for a month, or if you always dress formally, dress casually for the same period. If you discover a significant shift in income, dressing for success may be your *Midas Touch*.

Self-Help Strategies

In the blank spaces below, write down a list of this chapter's financial strategies, which may become your *Midas Touch*. Do not hesitate to include other self-help techniques that are not discussed here but may bring you prosperity nevertheless.

_____

_____

_____

_____

_____

_____

_____

_____

_____

_____

Part V

MONEY AND SPIRIT

CHAPTER TWENTY

The Power of Prayer

The financial strategies discussed in this chapter are based on the presupposition that there is an all-powerful and benevolent Supreme Being, who is genuinely interested in your welfare and desires to give you the best of everything. To inspire Him to bestow upon you His divine gifts, you need to treat God as you would a parent: acknowledge His divine authority, behave by His rules and properly ask for what you want in the form of a prayer.

Even though God has no gender, I find it easier for the purpose of writing to follow most common traditions and assign Him a male gender. If you are a follower of the Goddess, or if you believe in many gods, you can still use this chapter's material to achieve prosperity. In this case, you simply have to substitute the name of a deity that you believe in for the word "God" in the sample prayers.

His Glory Is Everlasting

The affirmations presented below affirm God's authority over your life, as well as His ability to provide you with unlimited financial prosperity. I learned these affirmations in Christian churches and Jewish synagogues, but they can also be adopted for any faith.

Divine power draws to me all that I need.
I am a child of God, and all that God has is mine.
I am a child of God, and I share in God's bounty.

The above affirmations are only examples. So, feel free to modify them any way you want, or create a few more of your own and write them down below.

_____
_____
_____
_____
_____
_____
_____
_____
_____
_____

Gratitude

Good parents are usually encouraged by their children's gratitude to give them extra gifts and provide them with more attention. Same parents may be discouraged by lack of gratitude, and therefore may withhold their attention and do less for the ungrateful child to teach this child to be grateful. If you believe that God is a loving parent you may treat him as such by expressing your gratitude in a prayer.

And here are a few expressions of gratitude that I have heard in churches and synagogues:

I am eternally grateful for all the wonderful gifts
that I receive from my divine Father.
God eternal, I am grateful for the gift of life.
I give thanks for complete and immediate fulfillment
of all my desires.
I am grateful for

_____ (fill in the blanks).

Command Ye Me

Once I listened to a sermon, discussing our divine right to ask God for anything we want. According to the minister, God gave us dominion over the earth. Therefore, we have the right and ability to make our own decisions on how things are supposed to be run here. To insure our ability to rule this planet in His name, God promised to grant our specific requests, which we may bring up to him as our prayers. Such prayers can be general or specific, depending on your needs. And here are a few examples of such prayers:

God, bring into my business prosperous clients,
who need my services and are able to pay
fair price for them.
God, bring into my life people and events
that would lead me to prosperity.
God, I am asking your help and guidance in
generating the annual income from my job
(or business) of _____ (Fill in blank.)

Feel free to modify these prayers any way you want, or write down a few of your own below.

_____
_____
_____
_____
_____
_____
_____
_____
_____
_____

Judge Not

According to most religious traditions, the function of judgment is performed by Divine Authority. Any of your attempts to pronounce judgment upon another fellow human will result in God's judgment upon you. Similarly, any of your attempts to punish another person, regardless of the severity of crime, will result in God's wrath upon you. According to many, if not all, mystical traditions, holding grudges against those who wronged you creates a powerful bond that will bind the victim and perpetrator alike. The only way to break this bond is by forgiveness. It is also important to forgive yourself for whatever transgression you have committed.

Here are a few affirmations and prayers of forgiveness:

> *God's forgiving love has set me free.*
> *God, I pray Thee to restore peace and understanding*
> *between me and* _____ (Fill in the blank.)
> *Father, forgive them. For they know not what they do.*
> *God has forgiven me all my sins, and restored*
> *His divine law in my life.*
> *Father, forgive me for* _____ (Fill in the blank.)

_____

_____

_____

_____

_____

_____

_____

_____

_____

_____

In addition to the above prayers, practice forgiveness in everyday life by avoiding any thoughts or deeds of judgment.

To the best of your ability, let go of resentment as well.

You may frequently fail at the beginning, but your ability to forgive will improve with practice. You may be doing a favor to the person whom you forgive, but you also are doing even a greater favor to yourself, since if you forgive, you may allow this imperfect person go out of your life forever.

Nine Steps to Prosperity

Here is a step-by-step process of using divine principles of prosperity in your life.

Step One. Make a decision on how much money you need to live a prosperous life. Be generous to yourself. Don't you believe that God is all-powerful?

Step Two. Create a collage, picturing the life you want to live in all details. Look at this collage daily. Every night before retiring, actively visualize its content in your mind. The picture on the collage is static, but you can set it in motion in your visualization, so it becomes like a movie.

Step Three. Combine your visualization with prayers and affirmations.

Step Four. Ask your loving Father what specific actions you have to take to manifest what you desire. God's advice may come to you in your dreams, or it may emerge as your own business decisions.

Step Five. Translate your ideas into a business plan.

Step Six. Begin implementing your plan into action.

Step Seven. Add affirmations and prayers of gratitude, geared toward achieving specific results, according to your business plan.

Step Eight. Join a local prayer group if possible. If not, create your own. At the very least, attend regular services at any religious or spiritual organization of your choice.

Step Nine. Adjust your plan of action, as well as your affirmations, visualization and collage, as you continue making progress on your journey to prosperity.

Note: I have to admit that the above steps were not revealed to me by God. Instead they were the result of my personal and professional experience. Therefore, feel free to modify them to fit your needs and personal preferences.

Love Conquers Everything

"God is love," one of the basic principles of Christianity, would be shared by most other religions, old and new. Applying this principle for prosperity may become your *Midas Touch*. The first step is to accept that God's love for his creation permeates this world and is the primal cause of its existence and evolution.

The next step is to visualize radiating God's love constantly, which might be similar to the visualization on radiating wealth from Chapter Nineteen. You can combine this visualization with affirmations or prayers. For example:

I radiate God's love now and always, here and everywhere. God, let me radiate Thy love.

Imagine sending rays of love to your potential clients, customers, bosses, supervisors and everyone else, who may be beneficial to you financially.

Express your gratitude to God, silently or verbally, for every payment that you receive, and bless every bill that you pay.

When customers or clients enter or leave your office, visualize sending them God's love coming from your heart.

Letter to God

Writing a letter to God is an easy matter. The only rule is that you must acknowledge His authority and ask for what you want. I deliberately do not provide any samples. What is coming from your heart will produce much greater effect than following any formula.

How to deliver your letter to God? Since God is everywhere, the delivery method is irrelevant to Him, but it may be relevant to you. So, send your letter to God in any way consistent with your faith. Consult your priest, minister or rabbi if in doubt.

Enlisting God's Help for Success

In the blank spaces below, write down a list of prayers and other religious and spiritual practices, which may help you to achieve prosperity. Do not hesitate to include any religious or spiritual practices not discussed here.

_____

_____

_____

_____

_____

_____

_____

_____

_____

Note: Even though your prosperity prayer may be your *Midas Touch,* frequently it is not enough. In addition to praying, you may still engage into other income producing activities to improve your financial situation.

CHAPTER TWENTY-ONE

The Metaphysical Approach

Most people believe that everything metaphysical is either a sham, or a play of imagination of confused minds, or—even worse—insanity. A small minority on the opposite end highly overrate the usefulness of metaphysical practices in everyday life, frequently hoping to manifest unlimited prosperity with very little knowledge of the subject and no effort whatsoever.

Both sides are only partially right, or partially wrong, depending on your personal preferences. I have experimented with some metaphysical practices myself and can testify that they can produce astounding results. Unfortunately, these practices can also produce undesirable side effects, but only in people already suffering from mental disturbances. Occasionally, such side effects may include an acute psychosis, as I observed while working as a clinician in a psychiatric emergency unit.

If you have a predisposition to schizophrenia or suffer from Borderline Personality Disorder, skip this chapter altogether, or at least proceed with great caution. However, for mentally and emotionally stable people, the strategies discussed here are perfectly safe. Nevertheless, stay away from Demonology depicted in *Buffy, the Vampire Slayer*.

Note 1: Besides being dangerous to your sanity, Demonology and other dark arts are useless in matters of prosperity. I encountered dozens of people who applied them for years with no results whatsoever.

Note 2: In all metaphysical matters, it is crucial that you do not discuss any of your practices with non-believers, unless they are open-minded, reasonable and supportive. However, try to solicit an honest opinion from those who are of like mind. Metaphysical practices are geared toward producing invisible, though dramatic, shifts inside your own psyche that will hopefully manifest in a desired transformation of your existing external conditions. This makes objective evaluation of the results of your practices especially difficult without the input and feedback of others.

Now, let me tell you about the metaphysical practices that I have tried myself and have heard about from my students and associates.

Numerology

According to numerology, every letter of the alphabet corresponds to a specific number, and by performing simple arithmetic with the letters for your name, you will come up with a primary number for your name. Each number corresponds to certain qualities of character, including your ability to generate income. You can also apply numerology to your birth date, your address, your car license plate, etc.

Case study: Joseph

Joseph borrowed a numerology book from a local library and, following the book's instructions, changed a few letters in his name. A 25% income increase soon followed.

* * *

I am aware that the above case is not a scientific proof that numerology works. However, I heard of enough similar cases to get convinced that it does work, at least for some people. I may even agree with the skeptics that in numerology and in many metaphysical practices such effects might be purely psychological, similar to a placebo effect. So what? If it works for whatever reason and does not produce negative side effects, use it.

If numerology is your *Midas Touch*, it will be easy to learn it and as easy to apply. I would still recommend that you consult a professional numerologist at least once. Otherwise, costly mistakes are likely.

You can find books on numerology in your local public library or in most bookstores. I personally prefer Norman Shine's *Numerology*.

The I Ching

The *Book of Changes*, or the *I Ching*, contains a system of various Chinese hexagrams and their interpretations. It can be used for guidance in all matters, including financial. The book can be found in most bookstores or public libraries. It is easy to use, and you can probably manage without consulting a specialist, even though such consultation can be helpful. Your chances of using the I Ching as your *Midas Touch* will be greater if it is a part of your heritage, and if you or any member of your family successfully used the *I Ching* to obtain advice on financial matters in the past.

Tarot Cards

Tarot cards have been used for fortune-telling since the Middle Ages. Below is an example on how they can be applied in financial matters.

Case study: Dan

Dan consulted a Tarot reader concerning his business plan to organize a New Age singles organization. He wanted to know if this business would bring him sufficient profit. The Death card came up in response to Dan's question. The reader interpreted the symbol of death on the card as transformation. However, the obvious interpretation of the Death card was correct, as future events confirmed. Dan lost money on his first two singles events. Only a few people attended his third one, heralding the death of his business right from the start.

* * *

If Tarot was helpful to you in the past, it may provide you with sound financial advice in the present. If you have no prior experience, Tarot will be easy to learn and as easy to apply, if it is indeed your *Midas Touch*. I would still recommend consulting a professional Tarot reader at least once.

Books on Tarot can be easily found in your local public library or in most bookstores. I like M. J. Abadie's *The Everything Tarot Book*.

Burning Candles

Here, you need at least two large candles, but three or four might be better. One candle is always white, and the others colored. The candle's color and design depend on the result that you want to achieve. The candle ritual consists of writing a list of the ritual's objectives, which can be done in the form of affirmations, discussed in the previous chapter. As you light the candles, you recite a prayer to a Supreme Being to help you manifest your dream into reality. Then you place your list under one of the candles, and let the candles burn until they burn out.

I conducted this ritual once. It felt mystical, and there was a positive shift in my life in response to my prayer, but this change was not significant. Perhaps I was inexperienced and did not conduct the ritual properly. However, this ritual did work for a few of my clients and associates. Perhaps, such a ritual was their *Midas Touch,* but unfortunately not mine.

I believe that in burning candles, as well as in most metaphysical practices, the intense desire for positive change is more important than following any prescribed ritual.

If you ever conducted a candle ritual in the past with inspiring results, your chances to use it to achieve prosperity would be higher. If you never tried using a candle ritual before, it won't hurt to try it at least once. Ask for books on the subject in your local metaphysical bookstore or search the internet for more information.

Witchcraft

Case study: Jean

Jean was a newspaper reporter who attended a class on witchcraft in a local Unitarian Church. A few weeks later, she published an article in the metropolitan newspaper that contained her personal experience with it. Skeptic as she was, Jean admitted conducting a Wiccan ritual following the class. The goal of her ritual, manifesting money, was not achieved. The ritual produced no change in her income. However, a few weeks later, Jean mailed her monthly credit card payment. Her check came back with a note, stating that her credit card company had no record of her two thousand dollar debt. Her debt had miraculously disappeared, and just one ritual had made her a couple of thousand dollars wealthier.

There might be two explanations for Jean's story. Maybe her luck occurred as the result of her credit card company's computer glitch, which accidentally occurred at the time of her ritual. Or maybe, by some miracle, her Wiccan ritual caused this computer glitch.

Unfortunately, in many metaphysical practices we can rarely establish the cause-effect relationship between such practices and their results. Nevertheless, various scientific research provide undeniable scientific evidence that at least some of these practices do produce results. (One of the best sources on the subject is Jeffrey Mishloff's *Roots of Consciousness.*)

Therefore, there is a possibility that Jean's success was not due to just a computer glitch. Perhaps, by practicing the Wiccan rituals, Jean discovered her mighty *Midas Touch*, with the earning potential of close to $1,000 per hour.

If you want to follow Jean's footsteps and conduct Goddess rituals to achieve prosperity, you can find information on the Wiccan religion in bookstores, public libraries or on the internet. This religion was not designed for solo practitioners, though. To conduct the rituals, as well as other practices of this religion, such as divinations and spells, try to find a group of the like-minded in your area.

Alchemy

I am an amateur on the subject of ancient religions, from the Egyptian to the Roman. Neither do I know much about medieval alchemy, the Kabbalah, gypsy magic, American Indian occult practices or the rituals of the Masonic Order. However, *Harry Potter* and a few more serious books on the such subjects, such as Jon Klimo's *Readings on Parapsychology,* have convinced me that all these traditions, old and modern, contain financial strategies that may have as much chance to become your *Midas Touch* as any other.

If you have experience in any of the above traditions, try a few of these practices for a limited period of time, a couple of months at most. If any of these magical practices is your *Midas Touch,* you will experience a significant shift in your income. Please note that your metaphysical practices may bring results through natural phenomenon, such as the computer glitch in the reporter's case above.

Be aware that *some occult traditions may border on Demonology and Black Magic, and therefore must be left alone.*

Precious Stones and Crystals

Metaphysical literature suggests the use of talismans, which usually are pieces of jewelry, custom made for particular individuals, to correct their bad luck, resolve personal problems and cause the desired life changes. Talismans are frequently used in the areas of health, love and money. The practice of using talismans for good fortune has existed since the dawn of time. In our age, most dismiss it as superstition, though a few claim that it does work. I would tend to agree with the latter, even though I have to admit that the effect of using such objects to increase income might be purely psychological. Regardless of your knowledge or ignorance about why and how this may or may not work, try it out if you are inclined to do so. Do your research however before putting on any talisman. If such things are as powerful as some claim, they have to be used with caution, and a wrong choice of a metal, stone or crystal, may do more harm than good.

Astrology

Currently, astrology has the reputation of a pseudo-science. Nevertheless, since the dawn of our civilization, men and women of power have employed astrologers to advise them on the timing and course of action. So, if you are interested in astrology, you would be in good company of kings, queens, popes, as well as presidents and their wives, including Ronald and Nancy Reagan, and Hilary Clinton.

There are four ways to make money with astrology. The most obvious, and usually the least profitable, is to become a professional astrologer, helping your client in making decisions for a fee. You can also use astrology in assessing your own earning potential in various occupations to make intelligent career choices. In addition, astrology can provide you with the most auspicious times for business transactions to increase profit and avoid financial disasters. And finally, astrology is rapidly gaining popularity in stock market forecasting.

Like all other metaphysical arts, astrology is frequently unkind to amateurs. So, if you are fascinated with astrology, and want to use it to make money, do your research and consult a professional astrologer before using this ancient art and science in making major financial decisions.

Charlatans

Many practitioners of metaphysical arts are honest professionals who do their best in giving you qualified advice. You have to beware of charlatans however, whom you can usually recognize by their outrageous claims.

Case study: Clementina

Young Clementina left a prestigious college, her wealthy parents and the comfortable life of the rich and well-educated for an obscure man twice her age. Soon after they married, her husband, well versed in different religions and fascinated with mysticism, proclaimed her God's messenger, able to channel information coming from her spirit guides.

Young, beautiful, vibrant, highly idealistic and very naive, Clementina seemed to radiate abundant positive energy, and soon a small circle of followers started attending her seances. Her innate acting abilities, great imagination and irresistible hypnotic voice transformed her seances into masterpieces of theatrical performance. Even those who did not believe in the messenger or the message still attended her channeling sessions just for the thrill of it.

Unfortunately, in spite of her superb performance which brought her success, recognition and the adoration of her followers, and in spite of her unshakable faith in herself, Clemetina's sprit guides' predictions always went astray. Her spirit guides were especially incompetent in financial matters. All Clementina's attempts in following their financial advice resulted in financial disasters. Thus, Clementina repeatedly lost substantial amounts of money from trading futures, unwise real estate acquisitions, and legally questionable business deals. Apparently, following her spirit guides was *not* Clementina's *Midas Touch*.

These persistent failures to manifest money by using metaphysical practices did not seem to make any lasting impression on Clementina. She even managed to explain away her financial disasters as caused by Dark Wizards, fallen angels, corrupt government, the Mafia, communist conspiracy and other forces of darkness. Amazingly, her followers believed her!

Clementina did manage to make huge profits though. She was extraordinary successful in soliciting donations. She also had exceptional abilities in selling her books and seminars, in which, among other things, she provided instructions on how to make money.

* * *

When you encounter such self-proclaimed masters of power and magic with their outrageous claims, just ask yourself: "Why do they have to advertise their services and charge fees? Wouldn't it be easier for them to manifest their own prosperity magically, instead of going through all the trouble that normal business operations require?" In addition, inquire if they actually follow their own formula to make money, or their income is derived by advising people like you.

Metaphysical Financial Strategies

In the blank spaces below, write down a list of the metaphysical practices that could possibly become your *Midas Touch*. Do not hesitate to include those not discussed in this chapter.

_____
_____
_____
_____
_____
_____
_____
_____
_____

Note: In many instances, the metaphysical financial strategies discussed here can only work if combined with other more conventional income-producing activities, such as improving your business or job performance, or investing in real estate.

Part VI

YOUR ROAD
TO PROSPERITY

CHAPTER TWENTY-TWO

Finally, What's Your Midas Touch?

Hopefully by now you have developed a few great ideas on how you can generate sufficient income with minimal effort. Most of my students come up with as many as ten such ideas, and rarely less than three. Only a couple of those ideas are candidates to become your *Midas Touch,* frequently only one. How to choose? Let's start with summarizing all the ideas for a *Midas Touch* that you have generated so far.

Step One. Summary Of Ideas

Write down below all the possibilities for your *Midas Touch* that you have come up with in the previous chapters. You may have noticed that you listed similar or identical ideas in different chapters of the book. For example, the idea that investing in real estate is your *Midas Touch* may have surfaced in Chapters Six, Seven and Ten. In cases like this, note how many times they have appeared. Such ideas have a greater likelihood to point to your *Midas Touch.*

Case study: Pauline

Pauline, a middle-aged interior designer, grouped her various ideas for a *Midas Touch* into the following categories:

Pauline's Step One
- employment as an interior designer (her profession)
- inheritance (2 times)
- investing in real estate
- investing in stocks
- buying and reselling antiques (3 times)

And here, write down the summary of your own ideas for your *Midas Touch*.

_____
_____
_____
_____
_____
_____
_____
_____
_____
_____
_____

Step Two. Specification

Some of your ideas listed above are quite specific. Include all of them in the list below. Other ideas may be too general. So, from each of these general ideas from your list above, come up with one or two specific jobs, careers, businesses or any other endeavors that you may consider as your possible *Midas Touch*. Keep the total number of these possibilities below twelve if you can. You can follow Pauline's example below.

Case study: Pauline

From the list of her ideas for a *Midas Touch* from Step One, Pauline developed the following specific ideas:

Pauline's Step Three

1. Finding employment as an interior designer.
2. Starting a consulting business in interior designing.
3. Using her social connections to get clients for her business.
4. Finding a business partner.
5. Providing writing, editing and advertising services related to her business.
6. Improving relationships with her relatives from whom she might inherit.
7. Investing in fixer-uppers, then fixing and reselling them.
8. Providing staging for residential and commercial real estate.
9. Investing in stocks.
10. Restoring antiques bought cheaply in garage sales or found in her relatives' junk storage, and reselling them.

Now, it is your turn to list your specific ideas for a *Midas Touch* in the blanks below.

_____

_____

_____

_____

_____

_____

_____

_____

_____

_____

Step Three. Setting Priorities

The only way to figure out which one of the endeavors from the above list is your *Midas Touch* is to try each of them out and see the results. Unfortunately, most of us are too busy with families and jobs and can only try one idea at a time. How to choose which one to explore first as your possible *Midas Touch?* You can base your decision on any factor most important for you. Here are some of the most common questions which my students asked themselves while prioritizing their choices:

- Which of the above endeavors have appeared more frequently in the previous chapters?
- Which of these endeavors is likely to produce the income I need in the shortest time with the least effort?
- Which of these endeavors is likely to invoke only minimal internal and external resistances for me? (You realize that they all will mobilize some resistances, don't you?)
- Which endeavors will create the least disruption to my present life? (Do not even try to discover a way to achieve prosperity without disrupting your present life. Sorry, it cannot be done.)
- Which of these endeavors will produce the greatest excitement and enjoyment in my life?
- With my present skills, education, experience, resources, personality, etc., which of the above endeavors am I able to explore now?

The above questions can help you to determine your priorities. You can also add to them a few of your own.

Step Four. Prioritizing

From the specific endeavors in Step Two above, choose 3-5 which you think have the greatest chances to become your *Midas Touch.* You can base your decision on your priorities determined on Step Three.

Here is Pauline's list:

Pauline's Step Four
1. Finding a business partner.
2. Improving relationships with her family members from whom she might inherit.
3. Investing in stocks.
4. Restoring antiques bought cheaply on garage sales or found in her relatives' junk storage, and reselling them.

Now, you can follow Pauline's example in identifying those ideas that you want to try first as your own possible *Midas Touch*. Write them down in the blanks below:

_____

_____

_____

_____

_____

_____

_____

_____

_____

_____

_____

_____

_____

_____

Step Five. Life Confirmations

Take the first item from the above possibilities of a *Midas Touch*, and list 8-10 possible actions to explore it. Such actions may include making contacts and inquiries, requesting information, talking to individuals who are already doing what you want to do, etc.

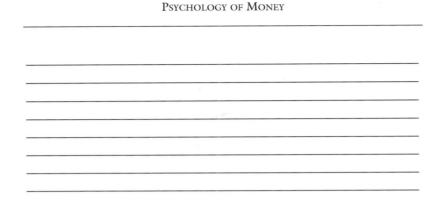

If your first choice of a *Midas Touch* is the right one, life will confirm it. Here are some signs to look for:

Confirmations for a *Midas Touch*
— beginner's luck
— the impression that life supports your effort
— the relative ease with which you accomplish your goals
— the relative ease with which you overcome the initial resistances
— the impression that everything you need on the road to prosperity comes to you by itself at the right time

The list of the above confirmations is provided for general guidelines only. These confirmations may vary from person to person, and by no means is this list complete. On your journey to prosperity, you will develop your own insight on what constitutes a confirmation that you are on the right path. Reading James Redfield's *Celestine Prophecy* or R. Hopke's *There Are no Accidents* will help you in this process.

However, if you make little or no progress and encounter serious resistances, then either your first choice is not your *Midas Touch* or it is not the right time for it.

A few words on timing. The *Midas Touch* is based on the principle that at least one of your innate talents can be used in generating significant income. This talent with income generating potential usually manifests in a variety of life paths. Hopefully you have identified most of them on the above list. Occasionally, due to external circumstances or your own inner psychic processes, one or several of these paths can be blocked. Nevertheless, a few other paths will remain open. Therefore, if your first choice does not work, go to the second choice on your list, and so on.

If you are attached to your first choice, try it out again in a few months. If it still does not work, let it go and focus on other choices. Explore your second choice in the same manner as you explored your first, and so on.

Once you discover your *Midas Touch* and start taking actions to implement it, you will be on your road to prosperity in a few months.

If life does not confirm any of the ideas from your list on Step Four—which is rare—go back to Step Three and choose the items that you have not chosen before. Repeat the process once again. The second time around it is usually, but not always, a charm. If it does not work the third time around—which is extremely rare—you probably need help, financial psychotherapy perhaps. It is also possible that you are stuck, and to get unstuck you have to apply the de-crystallization strategy described in Chapter Fourteen. You do not feel like going back through the pages? I understand. That is why I am reproducing the abbreviated and modified version on this strategy below.

Getting Unstuck

When you feel stuck, and all your monumental efforts produce only meager results, consider applying the process of de-crystallization, discussed in Chapter Fourteen. To refresh your memory, in de-crystallization you detach yourself temporarily from your familiar environment and, hopefully, from your familiar ways of perception. Vacations and retreats are the most common ways to get a fresh perspective on your life.

In many instances, a few days retreat to a quiet inspiring location will be enough. Stay solitary or surround yourself with the company of the like-minded. Review this book. Meditate. Pray for a vision. Record your dreams. Engage in sports, or do nothing. The most important point is that you engage in activities that you normally do not do at your business or home.

If you cannot get away even for a few days, take several half day vacations from your routine and engage in activities that you normally do not do, like traveling to a neighboring city, visiting a part of town you have never been to before, etc.

After de-crystallization, if successful, you will be open-minded and daring, full of new ideas, and ready to successfully implement them into practice.

And Finally, Your Midas Touch

Once you are reasonably sure that you have discovered your *Midas Touch,* write it out down below in large print. If you believe that you have discovered more than one *Midas Touch,* which happens frequently, list all of them here in large print in the order of importance. This list will be useful for you in Chapter Twenty-Four.

_____

_____

_____

_____

_____

Dysfunctional Strategies

In the blanks below, list the dysfunctional financial strategies of your family of origin that you may have identified in Chapters Six through Eight. Add to them the list of your own financially dysfunctional behaviors, including the dysfunctional strategies of power struggle, which you may find in Chapter Fifteen.

If you are aware of a few of faulty financial strategies you utilize that have not been identified through the processes presented in this book, include these strategies in the list below as well.

_____

_____

_____

_____

_____

In some instances, just being aware of the above dysfunctional strategies may stop you from unconsciously applying at least some of them. A few of these faulty strategies may cling to you, and it may take time and effort to get rid off them. Financial psychotherapy discussed in Chapter Fifteen is frequently the answer in severe cases. For everyone else, creating the adequate support group, discussed in the next chapter, will be enough to get you to apply your functional financial strategies and avoid the dysfunctional ones.

CHAPTER TWENTY-THREE

Resistance to Change

Unpleasant Surprises

The vast majority of people living on our planet are interested in money and would prefer more of it, usually a lot more. For many of us, having more money is not just a personal preference, but a powerful desire fueled by a perceived need. You may suppose that once you have discovered your *Midas Touch*, your actions to improve your financial situation will immediately follow. This is not always so. In spite of knowing exactly what has to be done to acquire wealth, many of us continue "business as usual" for quite a while, until a crisis puts a stop to it. Moreover, the realization that some of your financial strategies are dysfunctional may not automatically make you discard such strategies! You may continue applying them with full knowledge that they may lead to financial ruin.

If the above describes your situation, it does not mean that you are psychotic or neurotic, or that anything else is wrong with you. It only means that you are only human, and like all of us, you will have to overcome your own internal resistances to change. You will also have to struggle with the forces of human inertia, yours and that of those close to you. Your loved ones are very likely to resist your income increase, even though they may be the main beneficiaries of this change.

The Enemy Within

The mind has amazing qualities of forgetfulness and getting off course, especially when you are about to take actions that will produce internal anxieties. Such anxieties always arise when you attempt to change your life, and a significant increase in your income will surely cause such changes. Even if such a change is very positive and greatly desirable, anxieties will frequently arise. Psychologists label such anxieties as fears of success.

In early childhood, we all have developed various unconscious coping skills to deal with anxiety. Procrastination, "spacing out" and memory lapses are just a few of such strategies to avoid anxiety-producing situations. So, when you forget your *Midas Touch* for weeks, or delay its implementation for months, it is your mind playing tricks on you, trying to find a way out of the anxiety-producing situation.

The Enemy Without

Surprisingly, some of your loved ones will feel insecure about the positive change in your financial situation. Frequently, they resist your efforts to upgrade your lifestyle, even though such a change will benefit them as well. If this happens to you, do not blame your loved ones. It is not their fault. They are just victims of normal human tendencies, such as power struggle and fear of change. If you really have to blame someone, blame human nature instead.

As we discussed in Chapter Sixteen, a family or a dyad is a system that has to maintain the balance between its parts in order to exist. If one family member undergoes a significant change, the other family members usually attempt to prevent or at least resist this change. Such actions, directed at maintaining the family system's equilibrium, are usually unconscious.

Besides this unconscious resistance, your partner may also consciously struggle with your effort to make more money.

The partner who earns more usually has an advantage in a relationship power struggle. Unfortunately, this power struggle for real or imaginary advantages is a common feature of most relationships.

Be prepared that your partner may apply the strategies of demoralization, double messages and sabotage (all discussed in Chapter Sixteen) to get the upper hand in this power struggle with you. However, don't exaggerate the magnitude of this power struggle. In most instances, you will not have to divorce your spouse or separate from your partner to succeed. Most of this power struggle is motivated by instincts. Initially, your partner may instinctually try to prevent you from making more money in order to maintain his or her leadership position in the family. However, if you remain rock solid on your course toward financial success, the same instincts will compel your partner to either accept your leadership; or to make a considerable effort to increase his or her income, or achieve some other measure of success, to compete with you.

Note: This family dynamic discussed above affects not only your partner and the members of your family. It may also affect you. Yes, you may become the one resisting your partner's progress, while sincerely believing that you truly want him or her to succeed.

The Inertia of Conditioned Reflexes

Besides the above resistances, you may also have to deal with the inertia of your associations with your environment. You probably remember from school biology Pavlov's experiments with dogs. The dogs were conditioned to excrete gastric juices in response to the ringing of a bell. Like Pavlovian dogs, we have all developed a complex web of conditioned reflexes to our habitual environment, and everything around us compels us to respond automatically to external stimuli, and therefore continue "business as usual." Thus, the street signs in your neighborhood, the color of your bedroom walls, your favorite toothpaste, your clothes, the smell of your perfume or your shampoo, your toaster and almost everything else around you is connected through this web of conditioned reflexes. This web may reinforce your faulty financial strategies of the past, while preventing you from generating new ones which might lead to success.

The Inertia of Unconditioned Reflexes

Finally, there is also a biological inertia. All living organisms, humans included, are ruled by instincts and would not take action unless motivated by hunger, immediate danger, the strug-gle for power and domination or an urge to procreate. We are also motivated by curiosity, but in biological organisms this curiosity is of an immediate nature, rarely leading to any sus-tained actions.

Fortunately, you are not ruled by instincts alone, and are able to overcome the inertia of the conditioned as well as uncon-ditioned reflexes discussed above. However, it cannot be done without effort. The step-by-step process discussed in the next chapter will be the path of least resistance and minimal efforts that will significantly increase your chances for success.

CHAPTER TWENTY-FOUR

The Art of Manifesting

This chapter will discuss the path of least resistance to prosperity. On this path, you will be able to overcome the internal and external resistances discussed in the previous chapter, and learn to use the inertia of the mind to your advantage, instead of struggling against it.

Step One. Creating Reminders

Create a collage from old magazines and newspapers depicting the life you truly want to live once you achieve prosperity. Creating or buying a painting on the subject might be even a better option.

Once you have made a preliminary decision concerning your *Midas Touch,* spell it out below in large print. If you believe that you have more than one *Midas Touch,* which happens frequently, list all of them here in large print in order of importance, as you did in Chapter Twenty-Two.

_____

_____

_____

_____

_____

Now, include the above description in your collage, or attach it to your painting, and put it on your bedroom wall. Place it so that it will be the last thing you see before you fall asleep and the first thing upon awakening.

If your partner objects to this, place the collage or painting in your office or in some other place where looking at it will be unavoidable. There are no strict rules on how it should be done, except that your creativity is of primal importance here. So, to paraphrase Frank Sinatra, do it your way.

Besides this powerful reminder, you can also place various objects associated with wealth around your house or office. These objects may include dollar bills placed on your walls or a green dot on your car dashboard. Using affirmations and visualization as discussed in Chapter Nineteen may also help.

Step Two. De-crystallization

This is the third time when I encourage you to use the strategy of De-crystallization or getting unstuck, already discussed in Chapters Fourteen and Twenty-Two. This is indeed a very powerful strategy that can be used for multiple purposes throughout one's life. De-crystallization is one of the best ways to shatter the unconditioned reflexes associated with your habitual environment that may keep you stuck. Let's review briefly what de-crystallization is and how it can be applied here.

De-crystallization is a process of shattering the rigid familiar ways of perception. It can be achieved by detaching yourself temporarily from the routine of your everyday life. Relocation, traveling, pilgrimage, vacations and retreats are the best tools of de-crystallization.

If you cannot take a vacation, getting away even for a few days may be enough to develop a fresh outlook on life. If you cannot afford even a few day break, find 2-3 hours at least twice a week and engage in activities that you normally do not do. You can visit an unfamiliar part of town, eat in a restaurant you have never been before or read a book on a subject you have never cared about. What you do in these 2-3 hours does not matter, as long as you do something you have never done before.

You can also rearrange furniture in your home or office,

change your schedule, wear different clothes, etc. Change everything you can to detach yourself from the web of conditioned reflexes that have been ruling your life.

Quitting or changing jobs and terminating or restructuring relationships will also help you to de-crystallize, but such changes will produce significant stress. Therefore, do not quit your job or terminate your primary relationships capriciously and carefully weigh the effort/reward ratio here.

Step Three. Seeking A Guide

A qualified guide can be very valuable in helping you overcome resistances and inertia, and leading you on your road to prosperity. Ideally, you need a guide who has traveled the road that you want to travel, has overcome the obstacles that you have to overcome and is eager to lead you all the way, or at least as far as she or he has gone.

Let's hope that you are fortunate to find such a guide. However, you may have to get by with a guide who is far less than ideal, and you may have to change a few of these guides along the path.

Here are a few categories of individuals who can provide guidance on your path to prosperity:

Mentors are those who believe in your ability to significantly improve your life and are willing to help you to do so. They encourage you to take actions that may lead to prosperity. Unfortunately, they may have never been all the way where you want to go, and therefore cannot take you there. Most often, you can find your mentors among your grandparents, school teachers, priests, distant relatives and specialists in the field of your *Midas Touch*. Occasionally, your parents, spouses, lovers, close friends and even children can become your mentors.

Paid professionals are mentor substitutes, usually career counselors, psychotherapists or personal coaches who provide you with support, guidance and inspiration for a fee. They are great in the beginning of your journey to prosperity, but in the later stages their usefulness diminishes, and eventually they may depart from your life forever. The main functions of the paid professionals may include individual and family psychotherapy, career and financial counseling, and personal coaching. Ideally, they will lead you to your guides and masters, help you to form or find a support group, and take you to your *prosperity train,* which is discussed later in this chapter. You may have to settle with a lot less though.

The paid professionals' main limitation is that they must get paid to stay in business, which creates their financial dependency on you. This may significantly reduce the scope of their vision. A paid professional can rarely become your guide or master on your road to prosperity, except in rare cases when they have been traveling this road themselves and are already ahead of you. Even in this case however, their financial dependency on you can be a great handicap.

Ideal Guides are those with the *Midas Touch* identical or similar to yours, and who are able and willing to guide you all the way to prosperity. Like a mentor, your guide has a personal relationship with you, which is not based on paying a fee for services, as it is with the paid professionals. Unlike a mentor, who can only inspire you to take action, a guide has already made it as far on the journey to prosperity as you can only dream of going, and therefore knows what awaits you on every step of your own journey. The best way to find such a guide is to do what you must to continue your journey and be open to the possibility of meeting him or her. Remember that guides are not all-powerful or all-knowledgeable superior beings, but mere humans like you and I. They are just individuals able and willing to lead you where you need to go.

Story Tellers are guide substitutes. They create stories that inspire and guide you on your road to prosperity. Such stories are usually told in the form of a book or film, but also can be found in an inspirational lecture, class or seminar. At the moment, I am performing the function of a story teller in your life.

Masters are individuals who take you as an apprentice and work with you to develop and polish your professional skills and life strategies related to your *Midas Touch*. Masters are similar to guides. Both guide you on your journey to prosperity, but with a master you have a much closer personal and professional relationship. Thus, Sigmund Freud, the founder of psychoanalysis, was a master for Carl Jung, the founder of archetypal psychology. Far back in history, Julius Caesar was a master for the first Roman Emperor, Augustus.

When your training is complete, your master will encourage you to function independently.

It would be great to find such a master, but unless you have really good karma, do not count on it, especially in the beginning of your transformational journey. Most of those who achieved prosperity did so without a master. So take action, but be open to the possibility of meeting your master one day.

Keep it in mind that a master on your road to prosperity will be just a human being. Therefore, do not expect any superhuman qualities from him or her.

Charlatans are either paid professionals, or those who aspire to become ones. A typical charlatan claims to be your guide or master without having proper qualifications to perform such functions. They claim to possess special powers, special knowledge or special talents, but their special abilities are never as exalted as their claims. They also possess a combination of inferiority, superiority and persecution complexes. They are usually in desperate need of money, as much as possible, preferably up front. However, they will settle for emotional support, recognition, attention, love, sex or anything else they can get. At their best, charlatans may become Story Tellers, transcending their personal deficiencies through their stories. At worst, they are masters of manipulation who would suck you dry if you let them, just like Clementina discussed in Chapter Twenty-One.

So read their stories, if such stories are useful, or attend their lectures, if they inexpensive, but do not elevate them beyond their stature. Beware—getting too close to them may bring you financial and emotional ruin.

Guides and Their Substitutes

Since you are not going to wait for a perfect guide or master, list below the ones who can provide guidance and inspiration for you now, even though they may not be ideal.

Books or films:

_____

_____

_____

_____

_____

Individual, group or family counselors:

_____

_____

_____

_____

_____

Career or financial counselors:

_____

_____

_____

_____

_____

Personal coach (es):

_____

_____

_____

_____

_____

Mentor (s):

_____

_____

_____

_____

Guide (s):

_____

_____

_____

Master (s):

_____

_____

Others (not discussed in this chapter):

_____

_____

_____

_____

Step Four. Forming a Support Group

An adequate support group is crucial on your journey to prosperity not only because it provides you with emotional and logistic support, but also because of the challenges that your peers may present to your habitual way of thinking and doing. Besides, you can learn a lot about what works and what does not from people who are on the same stage of the journey as you are. A functional support group will soon create a new web of conditioned reflexes, associated with prosperity, thus counter-balancing the forces of inertia discussed in the previous chapter.

Your ideal support group would consist of several individuals bound by the same purpose, who possess a similar *Midas Touch*. Such a group can be formed from your classmates, while attending a professional school or training related to your *Midas Touch*. It can also be formed from your co-workers, if your job is related to your *Midas Touch*. If you own a business, your business partners or employees may become your support group. Frequently, it is possible to form a support group through your active participation in a professional association.

As was true with seeking your guide, you often have to settle with a support group that is less than ideal. In the beginning of your journey to prosperity, you may join an informal group of people who are also trying to change their lives, and hopefully are also interested in prosperity. You may also find a professional support group, run by a counselor, professional coach or a priest. Occasionally, you may have to join more than one of these groups for adequate support.

Your support group will rarely take more than a couple of hours a week, and your investment in it will pay a high interest in the immediate future.

In addition to other sources, you may find your support group either through your guide or guide substitutes, like your counselor, coach or mentor.

In many instances, your support group can be formed or found in various environments listed below. Please specify which one you may want to explore in the very near future.

Job or volunteer position:

_____

_____

_____

_____

_____

School or training:

_____

_____

_____

_____

_____

Professional associations:

_____

_____

_____

_____

_____

Religious or spiritual organizations:

_____

_____

_____

_____

_____

Personal and professional development seminars:

_____

_____

_____

_____

_____

Others (not discussed in this chapter):

_____

_____

_____

_____

_____

Step Five. Taking a Prosperity Train

The best way to achieve prosperity is to take a *prosperity train,* which means getting a job or starting a business related to your *Midas Touch.* Professional schools, positions of leadership in professional associations, volunteer positions, apprenticeship programs may also serve as *prosperity trains.* When riding such a train, you may do a lot or you may do nothing. Either way, the train will bring you to prosperity, but you will be better prepared for it and have more fun in the process if you are actively involved. Such trains automatically provide you with a guide, a support group of fellow passengers, and all the inspiration and challenges that you need to make your *Midas Touch* fully functional. Even your quarrels with fellow passengers may be useful by showing what to avoid on your journey.

Step Six. Confirmations

"And how do I know if I have taken the wrong train?" you may ask.

This happens. You may take somebody else's *prosperity train*. This train may be taking other people to their models of prosperity, but you may have to go in the opposite direction in order to develop your own *Midas Touch*. In this case, life events will force you out of this train, or you will find your journey too uncomfortable to bear and subsequently get off.

"And how do I know if I am riding the right train?" you may ask.

Here I will give you a brief summary of the Chapter Three on *beginner's luck*.

If you are practicing you *Midas Touch*, you will experience a curious phenomenon called *beginner's luck*, with which you will defy statistical probability and enjoy a high return for your efforts or investment from the start.

You may also experience *instantaneous expertise*. Here, with little or no training, you will perform at your new job or at your start-up business equally or better then seasoned professionals in the field.

Another signpost is that practicing your *Midas Touch* is rarely hard work, never boring, and is not difficult to do. Usually, but not always, while applying your *Midas Touch* you will also *enjoy the process,* not only the profits.

Step Seven. Troubleshooting

"How come I do everything by the book, and still do not make much money?" you may ask.

Nothing is wrong with you, or with me, or with the book. The problem is that almighty Life (or God, or the Lords of Karma, if you will) has conspired to improve your character and make you a better and happier person, all the while forcing you to develop your creative potential and resolve your family of origin issues.

Does this sound like too much? I agree with you, but this is how life is sometimes, and neither you nor I can change it.

Frequently to achieve some or all of the above, Life chooses money as a primary motivator. So, to comply with Life's demand for self-improvement, you may have to do one of the following:

If you are introverted, you may have to reach out into the world to practice your *Midas Touch*. Then, the financial strategies discussed in Chapters Fifteen and Nineteen through Twenty-One may be not enough for you. Supplement or substitute them with financial strategies that include actions and relationships.

The extroverted may have to look within and add some of the financial strategies discussed in Chapters Fifteen and Nineteen through Twenty-One.

You may have determined your *Midas Touch* correctly, but it isn't working because your basic psychological issues are in the way. Then you may have to resolve them first. (See Chapters Fifteen and Sixteen for details.)

Frequently, people cannot achieve financial success until they begin living their destiny. You might review Chapter Four for a brief introduction to matters of destiny, or read my other book, *Discover and Live Your Destiny,* which will be published in 2005.

It is also possible that your *Midas Touch* has nothing to do with having your own money. Instead, you might be able to use money, social connections and other resources of your family, friends and associates (see Chapters Nine and Twelve for details).

A small portion of my readers will never become rich, no matter what they do. If this is your case, do not blame me, blame God or the Lords of Karma instead. If you do not believe in such things, you can always blame your parents. Even in this case however, your *Midas Touch* can provide you with a com-

fortable life of personal freedom, with your basic needs provided for with a minimum of your effort. You may have to learn
to economize and live simply though.

And finally, the socio-economic and political conditions of
your life may make it impossible for you to discover or apply
your *Midas Touch*. In this case, do your best to escape to a place
of greater opportunity, or at least minimize negative conditions
first.

Epilogue

It has been fun talking to you, but according to my schedule your *prosperity train* is about to leave. Hurry up! I don't want to feel guilty by causing you to miss your train. Who knows when the next one will arrive?

Have a fun and pleasant journey, and may your destination be everything that you have imagined. And....

May the Force be with you.

You prefer *Star Trek?* Then....

Live long and prosper.

Bibliography

M.J. Abadie: *The Everything Tarot Book*
Richard Bach: *Illusions*
Richard Bandler and John Grinder: *Frogs into Princes* and *Structure of Magic*
Deepak Chopra: *The Seven Spiritual Laws of Success*
Dalton Conley: *Packing Order*
Charles Darso: *The Black Book*
Shakti Gawain: *Creative Visualization*
Master Lam Kam Ghuen: *Feng Shui Manual*
Susan Jones: *Family Therapy*
Napoleon Hill: *Think and Grow Rich*
Robert Hopke: *There Are no Accidents*
Jon Klimo: *Readings for Parapsychology*
Jon Klimo: *Channeling*
George Lakoff and Mark Johnson: *Metaphors We Live By*
Lucas film production: *Star Wars*
John Malloy: *Dress for Success*
Salvador Minuchin: *Families and Family Therapy*
Jeffrey Mishloff: *The Roots of Consciousness*
Macmilan and Free Press: *The Encyclopedia of Philosophy. vol. 2*
Catherine Ponder: *The Dynamic Laws of Prosperity*
James Redfield: *Celestine Prophecy*
J. K. Rowling: *Harry Potter*
Virginia Satir: *Conjoint Family Therapy*
Barbara Sher: *Wishcraft*
Noeman Shine: *Numerology*
Marsha Sinetar: *Do What You Love. The Money Will Follow*
Ilya Teplitsky: *Discover and Live Your Destiny*
David Wallin: *Money Matters in Psychotherapy*

About The Author

Ilya Julius Teplitsky, born in Odessa, Ukraine, is a licensed psychotherapist in private practice in Oakland, California. His credentials include two Master's Degrees, one in science and another in counseling psychology, and a license as a Marriage and Family Therapist.

Mr. Teplitsky teaches his courses *Psychology of Money* and *Discover Your Life Purpose* at various educational institutions in the San Francisco Bay Area. Since 1992, he has conducted hundreds of public presentations at various organizations, including the University of California at San Francisco and Berkeley, City College of San Francisco and the East Bay Association of Marriage and Family Therapists.

In his eighteen years of professional experience, Ilya has developed his own model of financial psychotherapy and career counseling, based on the concept that psychological issues are evolutionary forces in disguise and that their resolution may lead us to prosperity and to our unique mission in life.

For your comments or inquiries, contact the author at:

PSYCHOLOGY OF MONEY CONSULTING SERVICES
Ilya Teplitsky, MS, MA, MFT, (MFC 29308)
2868 Carmel Street, Oakland, CA 94602
Phone/fax: (510) 530-3855
website: www.psychologyofmoney.net
email: ilya@lanset.com

About The Editor

HAVE PEN, WILL TRAVEL—WRITING SERVICES

I. Editing, ghostwriting and developing non-fiction projects—articles, books & letters

II. The Art of the Memoir

Will Your Story Be Buried with You?
Hire A Personal Biographer and Create Your Own Personal Memoir

A Memoir is a Priceless Legacy to Leave Your Family and Friends

Through interviews and conversations I will help you write, edit and publish a unique personal document.

- I am a family therapist with 20+ years of experience
- I am also a published author, editor & ghostwriter

I can help you write your story & guide you through a journey of remembrance, bringing out the memories you wish to pass on.

George D. Cohen, LCSW
(510) 558-9130   gcohen1720@aol.com
El Cerrito, CA

TO ORDER BY MAIL

Name: _____

Address: _____

City: _____ State: _____

Zip: _____

Phone: _____

Email: _____

Book price: $15.99

Sales Tax: Please add 8.25% for shipping this book to California addresses.

Shipping and handling: Free

Total Enclosed: _____

Mail to: Ilya J. Teplitsky
2868 Carmel St
Oakland, CA 94602.